BA
An Insider's Guide

REBECCA JURY

AUCKLAND UNIVERSITY PRESS

First published 2012

Auckland University Press
University of Auckland
Private Bag 92019
Auckland 1142, New Zealand
www.press.auckland.ac.nz

ISBN 978 1 86940 577 9

National Library of New Zealand Cataloguing-in-Publication Data
Jury, Rebecca, 1987-
BA : an insider's guide / Rebecca Jury.
ISBN 978-1-86940-577-9
1. Study skills—Handbooks, manuals, etc. 2. College students—
New Zealand—Life skills guides. 2. Bachelor of arts degree—New Zealand.
I. Title
378.170281—dc 22

Cover design: Kalee Jackson

Printed in China by 1010 Printing International Ltd

Contents

Step 1
Want it

I've been there. It's a crazy, weird time as you try to plan your academic future. You've decided (or at least someone has decided) that you're going to university. Now you're on a 30-metre diving board and your university career is stretched out in front of you like an Olympic-sized swimming pool. Are you brave enough to take the plunge into this new world? Are you strong enough to be able to get to the other end? Is it worth the effort?

I've been on that board. I've taken the plunge. I've swum right down to the other end.

I'm remembering what I was thinking when it was me up there. Commitment. Money. Time. I'd just returned from my first OE and was painfully aware of what else fifteen grand could buy. I did a rough calculation of how many countries I could visit in the time it would take me to complete my degree and seriously considered recalling my enrolment. I was thinking about failure. What if I wasn't smart enough to do well at uni? What if all that commitment would be for nothing? What if my degree didn't get me anywhere? What if a Bachelor of Arts really did stand for Bugger All in the real world?

If you don't want an arts degree, stop now. Turn around, climb back down the ladder and come back another day. I can help you get a degree, but I can't make you want one in the first place.

If you do want one – great. Dive in now. Let's get started.

Make it official

Before we can go any further, you need to choose which university you want to go to. Choose it based on its reputation, its courses, where it is and who else is going there. Then choose a backup.

The next stage is letting them know you're interested. Call them now or go online to request an enrolment pack. Enrolling can be a long process so it's crucial to start the process off as early as possible – no commitment required, this is just the first point of contact.

Lodging your interest at two unis allows you to check them both out and then make an informed decision about which one is right for you. Plus, with entry requirements getting more selective, it pays for you to have a second option.

Handy links . . . for checking out unis online:

Auckland University of Technology
www.aut.ac.nz

Lincoln University
www.lincoln.ac.nz

Massey University
www.massey.ac.nz

The University of Auckland
www.auckland.ac.nz

University of Canterbury
www.canterbury.ac.nz

University of Otago
www.otago.ac.nz

University of Waikato
www.waikato.ac.nz

Victoria University of Wellington
www.victoria.ac.nz

Step 2
Plan it

Somewhere along the way, someone started spreading the word that a BA is the course to take if you don't know what to do, and that 'BA' actually stands for 'Bugger All' – bugger all effort and bugger all use to anyone. That person was right – on one level, at least. A BA is a very interesting way to spend your time if you don't know how else to spend it and, if you don't mind low and mediocre marks, requires bugger all effort. Consequently, if you've got no real reason to get a BA and if you're just scraping through in all your assignments, your BA will be worth bugger all to you at the end.

To those who know anything about it, though, a BA doesn't stand for bugger all. BA is short for Bachelor of Arts, an internationally recognised degree founded on ancient principles of education. Technically, a BA is a degree in liberal arts – that's anything in the social sciences from English, Sociology and Media to Languages, History and Geography. Broadly speaking, though, a BA is a degree in thinking, debating, researching and arguing. It's a degree that asks why and how as well as asking what, where, when and who. It's a degree that explores the questions humans have been posing about the world for thousands of years.

While people (often those enrolled in other degrees) do love to mock the BA, if you've got a clear reason for getting one and you do justice to that reason while you're at uni, it's going to be worth heaps to you at the end. I know this because I did, and mine is. My BA shows the world not only that I am familiar with the theories of my subject area, but also that I know how to argue for and against them. It shows that I can think at a tertiary level, that I can do so under pressure, and with great results. It shows that I was prepared to commit to the long journey of getting a degree.

At the end of your time as a student, your BA will reflect the effort you have invested in it. The first investment you should make into your degree is planning. And the first thing you need to plan out is your reason for bothering.

Find a reason – any reason – to study

Before you can get what you want, you need to know what you want. You want a degree, but why? Why a BA? Do you want a degree that will help you get your dream job? Or do you want one to get you into a postgrad course? Do you want to learn new things, expand your mind, see the world in a new light? Or are you after something tangible to show for your intelligence?

As a teenager, I was never set on the idea of university. I left high school singing my freedom from the institution of formal education and headed straight into the world on my OE. After a year of travel and café jobs, I was ready to look for a career. Having worked with my hands in one sink or another since I was thirteen, my requirements were simple: a career that would allow me to use my language skills in a way I found meaningful, to interact with people and to keep my hands dry. After a month of gazing enviously at job positions aimed at 'candidates with at least Bachelors-level qualifications', I enrolled at uni.

While my quest for a career was what pushed me into my degree, what pulled me in was my desire to learn. I love to learn and, while I maintain that life presents opportunities to learn wherever we go, nowhere teaches you *how* to learn better than university. Getting a degree hasn't made me a better person, but it has made me a better learner – someone who knows how to approach an issue in order to see all sides of the story, someone for whom every answer poses another three questions, someone who knows that learning is never finished.

I went to uni to make myself eligible for the sort of job I was jealous of other people for having; you will have your own reason for being there. What that reason is doesn't matter, as long as you have one and you totally believe in it. If you decide to work as hard as I did, your uni mates (and, in weak moments, yourself) will ask why you are bothering. If you truly believe in your reason your answer will dispel any doubts; mine was always 'because I want a transcript that proves to the world I'm the best person for the job'. No one ever tried to argue with that.

Not exactly sure what you want to achieve from your degree? Think ahead to the moment you are handed your certificate, the day you take it home and put it up on the wall, the day you see your name with letters after it. Will it make you feel proud? How will your life be different? What will your degree represent to you every time you look at it? Completing a degree is inspiring, energising, rewarding and, at times, painstaking. For me, retaining a mental image of my degree hanging on my office wall put both the highs and lows of uni into perspective.

I saw my degree as my doorway into the kind of job I wanted, although I didn't know exactly what job that was. If you're doing a degree with a certain job in mind, find some ads for it on Seek or Trade Me or talk to someone currently in the position. Then, before you enrol, plan out the CV you'd need to get that sort of job. If you've got a specific postgrad course in mind, get in touch with whoever runs it and ask what you'll need to get in. You'll probably find out (possibly for the first time) what a prerequisite is. If, like me, you don't have anything that specific in mind, keep your options open.

If you want a clearer picture of what you might use your BA for professionally, there's plenty of help on offer. Google will direct you to hundreds of 'career quizzes' that ask you a series of questions then suggest potential careers options. The New Zealand government's version of this is Career Quest, which asks you 78 questions before suggesting jobs that match your personality and strengths.

As well as online help, there are careers advisers at school and uni whose job it is to help you plan your future. If you don't know what you want to do, they can help you identify your interests, choose your courses and decide what jobs to aim for; if you do know, they can steer you towards the most useful courses and give you some nifty tips on what employers like to see.

As valuable as professional help is, a lot can also be gained from talking things through with the friends and family who know you the best.

Handy links . . . for checking out future jobs:

Seek – New Zealand's #1 Job Site
www.seek.co.nz

Trade Me – Where Kiwis Buy and Sell
www.trademe.co.nz

. . . for working out what you want to do with your life:

Career Quest
www2.careers.govt.nz/tools/careerquest

Work out how to enrol

Once you've found a reason to get a BA, you need to work out how to actually sign up for one. I never anticipated that this would involve so much choice. Having heard about people graduating with a 'BA in Sociology' or a 'BA in History', I figured that all enrolment would require me to do would be to tick the 'BA in English' box on a form, send it away and await my timetable of classes.

The enrolment 'handbook' that was delivered to me was so thick that the postman gave up trying to force it through the letterbox and left it on my doorstep. It had a smooth, glossy finish and this, along with the ecstatic-looking students on its cover, made me think that it was going to be an easy-reading guide to student life. I put on some Pink Floyd and went and sat in the sun with a beer to thumb through it.

As is my style, I opened the handbook to the middle and began to read. By the end of the first page I'd been consumed by a wave of jargon – 'course codes', 'points', 'levels' and 'EFTS' washing over my head as I sipped my beer and tried to make sense of it all. I quickly discovered that there was no prescribed 'BA in English' but a baffling array of courses from which I needed to construct my own.

Most courses were on offer in either 'Semester 1' or 'Semester 2', with some labelled 'Whole Year'. As I flicked back and forth between the calendar planner at the front and the courses in the middle, I learnt that the standard university year – generally running from February to November – is split into two semesters, which are broken up by a set of exams and then a short holiday. Semester 1 just meant the first half of the year,

Semester 2 the second. I decided not to worry about Summer School – Semester 3 or Trimester 3 at some unis – for now.

The 'degree structure' diagrams at the front of the book showed that only about a third of the courses I needed for a BA in English had to be from the English schedule. The rest could be split across other courses from the Arts schedule and courses from any other school of study.

Each course was given a 'points' value: my degree required that I complete a total number of points, including a certain number at 100 level, at 200 level and at 300 level. On closer inspection, the 'level' of each course corresponded to the year of my degree in which I was recommended to complete it – the majority of 100-level courses, for example, I was expected to complete in my first year of study, 200-level courses in my second year and 300-level courses in my third year.

To make matters more complicated, each course was referred to by a 'course code'. These codes were made up of a four-letter subject code (such as ENGL for English) and a three-digit number (such as 102), which indicated its level (ENGL102 being a 100-level course) and its particular identity (in this case 02 identified it as a classic English course: '101' is widely recognised as a subject's 'original' course).

Some 100-level courses had 'C's (co-requisite courses) that I *had* to take at the same time, and others had 'R's (restricted courses) that I *couldn't* take if I had taken courses with similar content. Under every 200- and 300-level course were the 'P's (prerequisite courses) I'd need to have passed before I could be accepted into the later courses. Finally, some had 'EQ's (equivalent courses), which covered the same material but under a different subject code. Your university will have its own set of codes, courses and cryptic numbers, so read your enrolment handbook carefully and find out what all the unclear terms mean.

Even though they provide uni advisers, open days and stacks of info on their websites, I believe that universities make the enrolment process as confusing as possible as a way of weeding out uncommitted students before they get onto campus. I can't think of any other reason for it. It took me the whole afternoon to fill in my enrolment form and by the time I was finished I was exhausted, the room silent and dark, my beer still two-thirds full beside me.

Plan a degree that suits your goal

Your first consideration is your major; like the title of a book, it will tell other people what your degree is about. Your major subject will reflect what job you want (so, for example, if you wanted to be a history teacher, you'd choose History as your major) and/or what you're most interested in learning more about.

Although a BA allows you to take a wide variety of courses in the first year, the further you progress, the more specific you get. So, while courses from your major subject might only take up a small part of your first-year schedule, by third year they'll be the majority of what you study.

A wide variety of 100-level courses means lots of scope to change your major. You might find that the subject you planned to major in isn't quite how you'd imagined it. No worries – provided you've got enough points in another subject, you can change your major at the end of your first year; I'd spread my 100-level courses out so strategically that by the end of mine I could choose between English, Mass Communication and Sociology.

The main things to bear in mind are the Ps, the prerequisite courses that you have to have passed, often at a certain grade, to be allowed into the next level of study in that subject. Some courses are compulsory if you are to achieve a major in that subject; in order to meet my first-year English major requirements, for example, I had to complete ENGL102 and one other 100-level English course. While choosing a wide variety of courses is all part of the fun of first year, do it in a way that will keep as many options open for you as possible in second year.

Craft your degree

My first high-school job was as a custom sandwich maker. For three years, I spent fifteen hours a week crafting whatever kind of sandwich my customers wanted. I made sandwiches with ten kinds of meat in them; I made sandwiches that were meat-free, dairy-free and gluten-free; I made sandwiches for invalids, babies and pets. With 2340 sandwich-making hours under my belt, I believe that I've made every kind of sandwich there is to make.

Planning your degree is like crafting a sandwich. The courses you have to take to meet your major requirements (like ENGL102 in my degree) are the bread of your degree; they are non-negotiable. Whether my customers liked white, wholegrain or gluten-free, they had to have bread – or else their meal was rung onto the till as a salad. Likewise, your BA will not be a BA unless you select the courses required to meet the required points for your major subject at each level.

While the courses you *need* to take are the bread of your sandwich, the courses you *choose* to take are its fillings – the meats, cheeses, salads and spreads. While I was required to take two first-year English courses for my major, I needed to take a total of eight first-year courses for my BA, leaving me with six to choose. These courses filled in the gaps of my English degree and in doing so turned it into a unique reflection of my tastes.

You may want to work towards a 'double major'. This gives you two areas of expertise but means that you'll have twice as many compulsory subjects. It also means that your degree will be partially ready-made. Your timetable may allow you to choose different elements but you'll have less creative licence over how it's crafted. Depending on who you are, you might find this a selling point or a turn-off.

If you're in the latter group, you can look at a 'minor' subject instead of a second major. A minor is like a major but you need slightly fewer points in it, allowing you to add another course or two of your choosing. Check to see if your uni offers or is planning to offer minors; Canterbury brought in minors mid-way through my degree, at which time I'd done enough Mass Communication courses to add one in at the last minute.

Whether you want a major, double major, or a major and a minor, write down the courses you're going to need to take to meet these requirements. You can only enrol in one-year's worth of courses at a time so make sure that the courses you choose for first year are going to get you into the ones you'll want to do later. Have some backups on hand in case the courses you want aren't offered in the year you want to take them: courses can get postponed or cancelled so it pays to have a couple of alternatives planned out just in case.

Choosing your courses

Once you've planned out the courses you *need* to take, start thinking about how you're going to fill in the gaps during your first year. What extras are you going to add so your degree is entirely suited to you? I always found this the most daunting part: to use the sandwich analogy again, anyone can make a basic sandwich but a personalised *gourmet* sandwich is something else.

I learnt that if you base your choices for first-year courses around the following five criteria, you can't really go wrong:

1. courses you need to do to get into second-year courses or for your major (most important);
2. courses you want to do (also very important);
3. courses you don't 'need' but that are relevant to the direction you want to go in (if you've got free spaces);
4. courses that seem interesting (provided you've put in place everything you need – some of the most rewarding courses I took at uni were chosen under this rationale);
5. courses that seem easy to you (although some of the courses I chose because they looked easy turned out to be challenging).

Most universities will allow you to credit a certain number of points from disciplines outside the Arts schedule to your BA. If you're interested, go for it; just bear in mind that studying a Law paper requires a different approach to studying for an Arts paper. I know a lot of people who studied in two disciplines at the same time while they were at uni and most of them think that it would have been much easier to do one at a time. On the other hand, some people enjoy the variety. It's a personal choice.

I'm not good with numbers, so every time I had to enrol in more courses I'd pay a visit to the course planning advisers at uni. These individuals have different names at different institutions, for example, at the University of Auckland they are called undergraduate academic advisers whereas at Massey they are student liaison advisers. All I had to tell them was what I wanted from my degree and they'd check to make sure that I was on the right track. When I decided that I might want to go into a post-graduate Journalism course, they suggested the courses that might help me get in. When I became totally confused by points requirements, they added mine up and assured me I was doing fine.

Overwhelmed by the responsibility of planning your life? Totally understandable: you're under a lot of pressure right now. Book a time with the people who get paid to relieve that pressure from you.

Admire your handiwork

You've crafted your degree. While you can enrol for only one year at a time, you have a plan for the subsequent years. No one else's plan is likely to be exactly the same as yours. This is one of the reasons why the BA is so popular – there is a wide variety of courses for you to choose from and there's a lot of flexibility over how you structure these courses into your degree.

Before each year of your degree, you'll need to enrol in a new set of courses – both compulsory and chosen. As you enrol in more compulsory courses for your major, you will accrue more layers; and as you enrol in more courses of your choosing, you will add in more and more pieces that are appealing to you and your purpose for various reasons. Your degree will take on its own shape and its own rationale.

Send it away

Mail in your enrolment form or hit 'enter' on the online form as soon as you can. Things get pretty hectic in the final weeks before the semester starts, so it's crucial you get all the paperwork in well before the cutoff date. Leaving it to the last minute means risking your place in the courses you've chosen so carefully. Missing the deadline means missing your chance to be a student at all.

Step 3
Get into debt

As soon as you've enrolled, your degree is your job. Your occupation is officially 'student'. By the way, you're not going to get paid for this job. Actually, you're going to have to pay to do it. Quite a lot. Before you can prepare academically for your courses, you need to work out what you're going to live on. You need to work out what you need. You need to work out how you're going to pay for it.

Studylink

Can't afford to study? Join the club. However, while you might be afraid of your new environment and you might feel insecure about your lack of academic know-how, in New Zealand you should never have to worry about how you're going to pay your fees. Ours is one of the few countries in the world where people lend us money to be students.

These people are Studylink – a service of the Ministry of Education set up to help you pay for your education. They'll pay you while you study on one condition: you pay them back once you stop. Studylink's interest-free loan allows you to borrow the money for your fees from them without paying any extra for the privilege (unlike, say, the bank would with a house mortgage). This loan gets transferred to Inland Revenue at the end of your degree and you pay it back as a proportion of everything you earn and, if you want to, in voluntary repayments. A word of warning, though: if you decide to go overseas after your degree, Inland Revenue will start charging you interest on your loan as soon as you've been out of New Zealand for six months.

If you want Studylink's help, ask for it asap. If you haven't already, call them when you get to the end of this chapter. The application process can take a while – especially in the final weeks before the semester begins.

Get an online Studylink account as soon as you can. By the time I got around to activating mine, I'd become used to waiting on hold for forty-five minutes every time I wanted to check on the status of my application. I had become adept at getting on with my day with a phone crushed to my cheek, a skill that has not in any way been useful to me since.

As well as your fees, you can apply for money to cover your living costs. If you're under 24, have no kids and your parents earn close to the average wage, you'll probably have to pay this money back. In this case, your living expenses loan will be lumped together with your loan for your course fees, creating an even bigger amount for you to pay off once you start working.

Some people don't have to pay it back, though. In this case, it's called a student allowance, a free injection of money each week to help you cover the costs of living. You might be eligible for the student allowance if:

- your parents earn less than the threshold combined income (check the website for this, as it changes frequently);
- you are supported by only one or neither of your parents; or
- you are 24 or over.

If you're under 24, have been financially independent for a number of years before enrolling at university and have parents who earn an average wage or higher, I feel your frustration. By the time I enrolled at uni, I'd been financially independent for two years; expecting my parents to be responsible for my living expenses just seemed crazy. Borrowing money for living expenses was an option, but the money I was borrowing for my course fees was freaking me out enough as it was. I chose to work part time for my living funds instead.

How much Studylink can help you will depend on your unique situation, so the best way of finding out is to get in touch directly with Studylink.

Handy link . . . for getting into debt:

Studylink
www.studylink.govt.nz
0800 88 99 00

The things you need

Kitting yourself out is one of the joys of being a student. All of a sudden you can 'need' stuff. You can spend money – or better still, have money spent on you – because you are investing in your future.

A place to live

As a student, you have lots of options for where to live. Which one suits you best will depend on who you are, where you are from, your family situation and how much money you have.

The first option is your parents' place. Food. Power. Cleanliness. Amenities. Cheap or no rent. It's an attractive option to many.

If it's not to you, though, don't worry. Maybe you're studying in a different city to the one your family lives in. Maybe you have the kind of parents who don't want you to stick around. Maybe you have the kind of parents with whom *you* don't want to stick around. Whatever, it's a good excuse to go flatting.

Lots of students opt for a shared flat. If you know a group looking for accommodation, you can scout out the rental market together and find something you can split the rent on. If you want to get to know your friends better, this is the way to do it (just be prepared for what you might learn).

When you head off flat hunting, look for properties close to or on a bus route to uni and with enough space to prevent you getting in each other's hair. A cheap, efficient source of heating and internet connections are also pretty crucial for students. As exciting as it is to find the ideal flat, make sure you read the fine print of the contract before you sign; check whether power, water and phone charges are included, what appliances are supplied, the length of time you're being bound to the place and whether, if it's relevant, you're allowed to smoke or keep pets.

If you are on your own, you can look out for ads for spare rooms in established flats; students are transient beings and tend to come and go from flats throughout the year, opening up vacancies for you as they do so. Make sure you get a chance to talk to the people you'll be living with *before* you move in; where you'll be living is important, but *who* you'll be living with is even more so.

In my experience, you can get a pretty good impression of potential flatmates after about ten minutes of conversation, provided you ask the right sorts of questions. Here are some of the key things you should find out about your flatmates before you decide to move in with them:

- The sort of personalities you'll be sharing the flat with, and whether these will fit with yours. Personalities tend to magnify when people share the same place, so any warning signals now should be paid close attention to.
- The vibe of the flat – party central, study haven, professional – and whether this fits with how you'd like to live.
- The relationships of the flatmates – whether they keep to themselves or hang out together. You may love the idea of shared meals and flat movie nights or you may prefer a more independent lifestyle.
- How they get on with their neighbours. Neighbourly disputes can really kill your enjoyment of a place.
- How the cleaning gets done – check to make sure it's shared out evenly. Run a mile if you hear 'Well, the last person who had your room usually did all the cleaning for us.'
- Whether they eat and shop together: how food is paid for and prepared.
- How they pay for rent and bills – you don't want to get into a situation where you have to keep covering other people's expenses.

Flatting is a life-changing experience but it's not a compulsory part of being a student. Having left home at seventeen, I felt that I'd 'done' student flats before I even got to uni. During Year 13, I lived with four uni students in a dilapidated villa halfway between a liquor store and a night shelter for homeless men. After checking in to the shelter and trekking down to the liquor store, these guys would often stop outside our place to consume their purchases. At least once a week I'd find one or two crashed out on our porch and I'd prod them gently back to life on my way to school.

After sharing a couple of other student flats, I put my stuff into storage and headed to Europe with my boyfriend Blake. Here we lived out of backpacks and slept in tents, dorms and caravans. While our 'homes' were rough, they were our own; and by the time we got back to New Zealand the thought of sharing with others had lost all appeal. Finding a small two-bedroom place in town worked for both of us.

If you've got a bit more cash to spend or you already live with someone, a small place has a lot of perks. While you don't get the hectic, social fun of a shared flat, you get a quiet place to study, more personal space to spread your stuff out, and the ability to go out to party and then come home to sleep, rather than trying to sleep through your flatmates' shenanigans.

Another option is the uni halls, where you can either get your own room or a shared apartment. The plusses are huge: close to uni, reasonable price, plenty of other students around to hang out with – just remember to apply in time. The only potential downside is the fact that you have no real escape from uni life but, then again, that might be a plus for you as well.

Where and how you live while you're at uni is totally up to you. Not everyone who shares a student flat wakes up to strange guys sleeping on the porch, but some wake up to far worse. Choose a place that fits with who you are, how you study best and what sort of surprises you're prepared to face in the morning.

Handy links . . . for accommodation:

Flats

Free searches for flatmates and flats:
www.easyroommate.co.nz
www.flatfinder.co.nz
www.nzflatmates.co.nz

Uni Halls of Residence

Auckland University of Technology
www.aut.ac.nz/being-a-student/current-postgraduates/accommodation/campus-accommodation

Lincoln University
www.lincoln.ac.nz/services-facilities-and-support/accommodation

Massey University
www.massey.ac.nz/massey/admission/accommodation

The University of Auckland
www.accommodation.auckland.ac.nz/uoa

University of Canterbury
www.canterbury.ac.nz/accom/halls/

University of Otago
www.otago.ac.nz/about/accommodation/residentialcolleges.html

University of Waikato
www.waikato.ac.nz/students/accommodation/on-campus.shtml

Victoria University of Wellington
www.victoria.ac.nz/accommodation/halls/index.aspx

A study space

As well as a place to live, you need a place to study; these may well not be in the same building. If you have a spare room – great. If all you have spare is a corner, use that. If you live in the sort of flat in which you'd be more likely to find a money tree than a quiet moment to yourself, get a study space somewhere else.

While living at your parents' place may not be an option, studying there might be. If not, your local or uni library will have plenty of quiet corners that you can take over – some people work better away from the temptations of the fridge and TV anyway. Wherever you choose, it needs to be quiet and comfortable. It needs to be yours.

During my degree Blake and I lived in one of four damp art deco-style apartments in a looming weatherboard house opposite the Christchurch Town Hall. The insides of the windows were constantly wet and if I wore high heels in the bathroom they'd go through the floor. Despite this, it was a funky shade of green and, most importantly, had a spare room that overlooked the Avon River, Colombo Street and a council-maintained garden.

In this room, I set up a desk for my computer and a set of shelves for my textbooks and notes. The desk was an old kit-set one from Blake's uni days. I found the shelves in our apartment's shared laundry – a rotting shed in the driveway that had become a dumping ground for departing tenants and a useful source of odds and ends for new arrivals. If you don't have a shared laundry, the online equivalent is Trade Me; here you'll be able to find a computer desk for a couple of bucks and some bookshelves on $1 reserve. Some cities also have an inorganic waste day when people leave furniture out on the streets for others to take away – and rubbish collectors to vie for – so make sure you get there first. And check out ads for free or cheap furniture in shop windows and on supermarket noticeboards.

I put a couple of plants on the windowsill (good feng shui, I had read) and positioned a green armchair in the corner. I moved my book collection in from the bedroom to give a more scholarly feel. Blake bought me an ergonomic kneeling chair (Google it) from a garage sale for $2, which I slid under the kit-set desk.

On this chair, in this study space, I lived most of my life for the next two years.

Handy links . . . for cheap furniture:

Secondhand.co.nz, New Zealand's Marketplace
http://furniture-and-decor.secondhand.co.nz

Trade Me – Where Kiwis Buy and Sell
www.trademe.co.nz

Transport

Before you can attend university, you have to be able to get there. You need the kind of transport that makes it easy for you to get to all your classes, even that rogue one-hour tutorial on a Friday afternoon. You need to have a foolproof system for getting yourself to exams that includes several backups.

The most reliable source of transport is always you: if you live within walking distance of uni, getting to campus shouldn't pose you any challenges that a good pair of shoes and an umbrella can't fix.

Being close to uni isn't everything, though, and for many kiwi students it's just not possible. If you find the perfect flat with the perfect flatmates and the perfect price, there's no need to discount it because you can't walk to your classes. The apartment Blake and I lived in that was a good seven kilometres from uni and I never felt the need to move closer. In fact, the more serious I got about my job of being a student, the more I valued having a bit of distance between my home and my 'workplace'.

If you can't walk to uni but you can park within walking distance, think about getting a car. If not, public transport is fine – though not as cheap as it used to be. Whatever your choices are, choose the easiest one; the more difficult, time-consuming and expensive it is for you to get to uni, the less motivated you'll be to go. If a car is a viable option for you, the ideal sort is small, cheap to run and as new as you can afford. You can't go wrong with a late-90s Honda or Toyota. Check out *The Dog and Lemon Guide* for the most reliable makes and years.

More reliable still is a bicycle. Cheap to run, simple to fix, easy to store – this was my main form of transport. Having no garage, I stored it vertically, propped up on its back wheel in the hot-water cupboard. My backup plan if it was raining or if my bike had a flat tyre was the bus. My third option, should I miss the bus, was the car, a 1964 Mercedes-Benz 220SE which drained more fuel just in starting up than most small, new cars use in a week. My fourth option, should the Merc be out of action or break down on the way to uni, was a taxi. I always kept taxi numbers in my cellphone and a $20 note hidden in my wallet, just in case this happened on an exam day. Luckily, I never had to use them.

One of the things you'll need to buy if you have a bike is a padlock of some sort – you don't want your bike to be the uni packhorse, used at random, left wherever, and never where you need it to be when it's your main mode of transport.

Scope out your cheapest, easiest and most reliable transport option, then identify your backup plans. Aim to establish a straightforward, enjoyable way for you to get to your lectures and a series of foolproof strategies for getting you there if that one fails.

Handy link . . . for checking out cars:

www.dogandlemon.com

Computer

The computers available at uni for student use are not ideal. It's not a case of quality – most universities try to keep their computers relatively up-to-date. There just are never enough of them. This is not a problem if you want to check the news or browse your emails – if what you want to do is non-essential, there will be plenty of computers free. Any time you really need to use one, though, you can guarantee that there won't be an unoccupied computer chair on campus. Even the secret computers in corners and alcoves of the upper library floors – free on every other day this semester – will be in use when you need them.

Some of the most frustrating hours of my life have been spent waiting in lines to print off essays, watching as other students update their Facebook profiles, scan Stuff for news or send lengthy emails to their friends – the very things I do when I'm not in a hurry. And you can guarantee that when you *do* get to the front of the line the computer will crash, and then when you get a computer that works it will be logged in as someone else, and then when you get logged in your printing account will be out of money . . .

I lost count of how many times I ended up in this scenario, sprinting to the printing centre, thrusting my pen drive and handfuls of change at the boy behind the counter and shouting, near hysterical, 'I need this printed! Now!' before running to the essay dropbox, satchel flying, to deliver the essay with only seconds to spare.

Uni computers are stressful and, as a student, undue stress must be avoided. Doing so means, if you can afford it, buying a computer of your own. If you can't, Studylink may loan you the money to purchase one under 'course-related costs'. If not, ask your parents for a loan. If not, work in a temporary job until you can afford one.

Beyond saving you stress, it's a smart investment. If you have to bike or walk to uni every time you want to check your emails, a laptop will save you huge amounts of time and energy. If you drive or catch a bus, you'll probably find that the price of a modest laptop (getting cheaper by the week) is minimal compared to the cost of petrol or bus fares (getting more expensive by the week) over three years. You'll get your money's worth. For the next few years, you will spend the majority of your life staring at its screen. It is something you need.

Data storage

You need to back up your work. Trust me on this one. I used a combination of a USB drive and a G-mail account. After every work session, I'd save the document I'd been working on to my laptop, upload it to my USB drive and attach it to an email to myself. If I was leaving my laptop at home, I'd take the pen drive to uni with me. If I needed to take my laptop, I'd leave the pen drive at home. This, combined with the internationally accessible nature of my G-mail account, meant that my work was always saved in three places at once.

The day before our first essay was due I told the guy I sat next to in COMS about this tactic. He laughed and told me I had OCD.

When he stumbled into our 4 o'clock class the next day, his face was grey. Sometime during the night, his hard drive had crashed. Uni had refused to give him an extension, claiming that it was his responsibility to back up his work; he'd had to write his entire essay again and hand it in four hours late.

I may have got the last laugh on that day but I broke my own rule on more than one occasion and paid the price every time. Once G-mail didn't let me send an attachment from a uni computer; the one time I relied solely on my pen drive it failed as soon as I got it home. Once I stayed up working on an essay until 3 a.m., by which time I was so tired that I forgot to back up my work at all. As I was eating breakfast later that morning a virus consumed my laptop and I had to spend the rest of the day typing the essay from scratch.

If you don't have a universally accessible email account or if your account has limited storage, free web-based file hosting services like Dropbox allow you to upload and store your files online. If you don't want to use a pen drive, you can pick up an external hard drive pretty cheaply from your local electronics store. If you're really old school, CDs or DVDs still do the job. Use whatever you need to but always, ALWAYS ensure that your work is saved in three separate locations.

Handy links . . . for file storage:

Dropbox
www.dropbox.com

. . . for cheap electronic bits with free shipping:

www.miniinthebox.com

Stationery

How many other stationery bits you need is up to you. Personally, I enjoy stationery and soon found myself needing to invest in my future by way of rollerball pens, packs of highlighters and colourful ringbinders. Some people like to buy exercise books for each course but I didn't fancy lugging all of my notes around on my bike; instead, I carried a pad of refill and a pen in my satchel and transferred my notes into ringbinders once I got home every day. Some days I took my laptop but I never remembered the things I typed as well as the things I wrote down.

It sounds kind of lame, but nice pens are important. As I discuss later on, finding the motivation to take good notes an hour and a half into a two-hour lecture can be difficult, and having a decent pen to write with can make all the difference. You're getting your degree for a very good reason – now do that reason justice with decent equipment.

When you've got all the things you need, you're ready to go to uni.

Step 4
Be afraid

Uni is terrifying. Let's just get that out there. It's about a thousand times bigger than school, with a thousand times more people. As daunting as it had been moving from the security of Governors Bay School (then a full primary with about 100 students) to Cashmere High (the second-biggest high school in Christchurch), moving from high school to uni was scarier. It was like moving from Kaitaia to Auckland. Uni was a new city with shops and bars and gyms and cafés and doctors' clinics. It had thousands of inhabitants – some of them very, very smart.

Uni's status as a small city makes it a great leveller. If you really did have to move from Kaitaia to Auckland to attend university, rest assured that there are no 'locals' amongst first-year students. Everyone is new. Everyone is finding their way.

Like any good citizen of the twenty-first century, I began my exploration of this new city online. I went to the University of Canterbury's website and clicked into the section for 'students'. That was me now. I had a look at library details and course information. I clicked on a journal database.

What would I like to search for? On the desk in front of me was the enrolment handbook, open to the list of Sociology courses being offered that year. The course I'd circled was dominated by the word 'globalisation' – a term I'd not come across before. I typed it in. My search returned 186,806 journal articles about globalisation. I clicked on the first one and was taken to an online version of 'Globalizations' by B. de S. Santos. I read.

> What is generally called globalization is a vast social field in which hegemonic or dominant social groups, states, interests and ideologies collide with counter-hegemonic or

> subordinate social groups, states, interests and ideologies on a world scale.

To my mortification, I realised that I was less informed about globalisation than before I'd hit search. This onslaught of academic jargon had stripped my brain of more than it had added. Hegemonic? Ideologies? Counter-hegemonic? Subordinate social groups? Here I was, about to apply to enter an entire course about globalisation and I couldn't even understand the definition of the word. I was a Bieber fan at a Metallica concert. Someone's mum at a flat party. A pink umbrella in a pint of Guinness. I was a foreigner. I did not belong.

Feeling stupid

Feeling stupid is the first thing you have to be wary of. Size-wise, uni is a small city but conceptually it's another world. The language is designed to make everything sound complicated; this is generally achieved by adding '-isation', '-emonic' or '-ology' on the end of everything. Globalisation is basically the process of ideas and organisations becoming globally significant – like how McDonald's has spread across every continent in the world bar Antarctica. You'd be hard-pressed to find a journal that will word it this simply, though, because simple is not the way it's done in the academic world.

I'll talk more about this later – all you need to remember now is that if this is your first time at university you're going to feel ignorant about a lot of things and that's perfectly okay. The ideas aren't above you, they're just unfamiliar to you. You are not stupid, you are just new.

Getting lost

Overwhelmed by the online world of uni, I headed to campus to see if I could make more sense of things on the ground. I took with me romantic notions of strolling about an American-looking campus, clutching a glossy textbook against my chest and soaking up the intellectual vibe of the place.

After five minutes I was lost. After fifteen minutes I was hot. By twenty, I was starting to worry that I might never see the horizon again. Half an hour in I reached a courtyard with a big stand labelled 'location board' at its centre; this I made a beeline for and seized with both hands.

Laid before me was the plan for a small city, dotted with parks, bus stops and cafés, broken up by rivers and main roads, irregular rooftops packed together like the product of some giant uncoordinated game of Tetris. These buildings were dissected into three main blocks by Waimairi Road and Ilam Road. None of the blocks seemed to resemble where I'd spent my morning.

I made a little walking man with my fingers and tried to retrace my route on the map. A crowd of guys walked past and sniggered. As they crossed the courtyard, one of them turned and yelled over his shoulder: 'Riccarton High's that way, loser!'

I ditched the map and kept walking. Every building I came to seemed grey and imposing, every billboard scarred with graffiti. I knew I'd left my bike near the main library – if I could only find my way back there, I'd be fine. I reached a tiled area and, in desperation, approached an elderly guy sitting on a bench.

I smiled apologetically.

'Sorry to be a pain, but could you please point me in the direction of the library? I'm totally lost.'

He returned my smile and pointed over my shoulder to the building behind me. The one with the massive 'Library' sign.

'Do me a favour,' he said. 'Get a map.'

I cycled home, defeated. My first day on campus had not been the liberating experience I had hoped for. I felt like a try-hard, struggling to fit into a world that was clearly out of my league. I felt dumb. Worse than anything, though, I felt totally, thoroughly uncool.

I returned to the uni website, found a map and printed it off. This I carried with me for most of my first year of uni. I kept it inside a book and pretended to be one of those people who gets so engrossed in their reading that they can't even put it down to walk. (No one ever batted an eyelid. At uni, it's more socially acceptable to be this sort of person than the sort of person who reads a map in public.)

The first time you go to uni with your print-out map, go on a weekend. Walk to every main theatre block. Walk between every main theatre block. If you know which theatres your lectures will be in, practise getting between them in about ten minutes, the amount of time you usually have between lectures. Walk to the library. Take a ride in the lift. Find the registry. Seek out the bookshop and browse the shelves. Find the health centre, the student association, the information centre, the recreation centre and any other centres that may be useful to you. Check out the selection of cafés on campus. Find the bar.

Explore on a day when you've got nothing much else to do. Take your time and allow yourself to get lost – this is a whole new world, remember, so it's understandable for you to feel overwhelmed. If you're seriously lost, just ask someone to direct you back to a landmark you know, like the library. While they may sound dismissive, chances are, they've been in your position before and are secretly just glad that it's someone else's turn to get lost.

Step 5
Get good habits

Now that you've got the things you need and know your way around, you've got a job to get on with. Your contract started from the moment you enrolled. It will last until you fulfil your whole reason for being here. The good news is that your job description won't change much for the rest of your time at uni. Although the content and difficulty of what you study will vary, your responsibilities will be largely the same from course to course and from level to level. Establishing good habits early will allow you to do well not just across all your courses, but also across the rest of your years at uni.

Your job description

Before you can work out how to do well in your student job, you need to know exactly what that job entails. Because every student gets involved in different things at uni, each student's experience is unique. At the same time, though, some responsibilities are common to *all* BA students. You'll need to attend your lectures, go to your tutorials, do your reading (both required and your own), complete your assignments on time and sit your exams. You'll also need to know who you can talk to if you have questions or problems, how to use the library, and how to take part as fully as you can in the life of the university.

Lectures

Lectures are the core of a BA. In first year, they're usually very different from classes at school. They tend to be huge, for a start. Most lectures take place in cavernous 'theatres' in which students sit in tiered seating and a lecturer stands up the front and facilitates a PowerPoint presentation. The lecturer talks, the students take notes and, for the most part, there's little discussion. Some lecturers like to ask questions, but in a huge theatre, answering is a bit awkward and tends to be dominated by one or two outspoken students. Most lectures run for an hour, some for two and a few for three. You generally have about two to four hours of lectures for each course per week. In first year, you might take four courses at a time, but in third year you might take only two.

The further you progress through uni, the fewer people you'll have in your lectures and the more discussion happens within them. Sometimes you'll be lucky enough to get small classes in first year, which operate a bit like tutorials.

Tutorials

Tutorials are more like classrooms. Most first-year courses run a tutorial timetable alongside the lecture timetable, requiring you to attend one tutorial for every week's worth of lectures. While lectures will be run by lecturers, most of whom either have a PhD in their area of expertise or are working towards one, tutorials are usually run by Honours or Masters students (the next steps after Bachelors) or by part-time tutors.

Where students are there to listen and take notes in first-year lectures, they're there to contribute in tutorials. It's your tutor's job to foster discussions about the course work and remind you to keep up with the lectures, readings, main theories and assessment. Often, your tutor will mark your essays.

In the interests of cost-cutting, funding may not be set aside for a tutor for your course. If this happens, lecturers may choose to run their own tutorials; if not, any questions you have may be restricted to lecturers' office hours, snatched moments between classes and emails. In my experience, third-year tutorials were the first to go, presumably because by then we were thought to be a bit more independent.

Readings

For every lecture, your lecturer will set chapters and articles for you to read in advance. These are the 'set readings', the ones that you have to read and be able to show you understand in your essays and exams; your tutor will usually help you with these readings in tutorials. There are often readings to do for tutorial discussion as well. As well as the set readings, you're expected to read stuff you find yourself – journal articles, online sources and library books that allow you to build your understanding on your own terms.

Essays and exams

Standard assessment for a BA course is two essays and a final exam, although some courses offer tests (in-class or take home) or extra research assignments as alternatives. It's up to the lecturers how they distribute the marks – those who use an exam usually give you the opportunity to complete at least 50 per cent of the assessment before you sit the exam; it's common for each essay to be ascribed 25 or 30 per cent of your total grade for the course and the final exam 40 or 50 per cent.

Your essays are designed to show that you can put together a structured answer to a specific question about a topic, using evidence from articles and chapters you've read to back up your points. Exams are designed to show how well you've grasped and remembered the key ideas of the course, and how well you're able to use what you've learnt to answer a range of unfamiliar questions. You're also assessed on how well you can put these ideas into a structured argument – usually in essay form, but sometimes short answer or, more rarely, multi-choice.

Excelling at your job

Attending lectures, going to tutorials, reading articles, writing essays and sitting exams are the five main requirements of your job as a BA student. How to do well at them? Everyone knows that it's good to study hard and get good results. But how, exactly?

Doing well is actually very simple, it's just that most students don't cotton on to it until they're in their final year. This is the time when many students start making the most of their courses and, in doing so, finding out that they *can* actually get good grades. Their success, though, is bittersweet; sure, their 300-level grades are great, but what about their earlier results? They *can* do well at uni, so why has it taken them so long to find this out?

Many people I have talked to believe that this frustration is key to the student experience. It's almost as if learning how to study at the *start* of your degree is cheating. To me, this is like saying that pilots shouldn't be taught how to fly before getting behind the controls of a passenger plane, or that surgeons should learn the basics of operating through their own trial and error on patients. A BA is a highly technical job, and students should be offered training both before they start and at the very beginning.

The less time you have to spend finding out how to do your job means the more time you can spend actually doing it. More time for meaningful study means more time to learn the core concepts and theories of your BA. The sooner you can start learning these, the sooner you can start learning how to challenge, support, compare and contrast them.

It's not about getting top grades all the time. It's about being able to look back on your degree at the end of it all and tell yourself that you made the most of every course you took. If you want to do the best you can right from the start, you need to get good habits now, by using both your own resources and those of the institution you've chosen to be part of – the university.

Good habit 1: Be nerdy

Before you put the book down, let me just remind you that being a nerd means something different when you're at uni. I know that at high school it's something you'd never want to be accused of. I know that there, being labelled a 'nerd' has devastating consequences for your social life and can sentence you to years of jeers and taunts, lonely lunchtimes and thrown apples.

Things change when you get to uni. Students no longer feel the need to shoot down their successful or hardworking peers, probably because there are a lot more of them. According to the 2006 census, only 11.2 per cent of New Zealanders have a Bachelors degree, suggesting that only the nerdiest of the population actually get to university in the first place. Uni is a place where the nerds of the world band together to form a majority, where it's the slackers who are hassled and those who get the grades are admired.

What this means is that if you were the kind of person who used to hassle nerds in high school, you might want to change your tack. You're now surrounded by people who have *chosen* to stay at school, who think it's cool to get an education and who have a vested interest in working hard. At uni, the nerd is no longer the person to pick on; the nerd is the person you want to be.

If you're the kind of person who used to get hassled for being a nerd in high school, you're going to have to adjust as well. You're probably used to being the top of your game, the best in the class, the big fish in the small pond. Well, that pond has just turned into an ocean, and you're still the same fish. What's more, there are hundreds, thousands more fish the same size as you, many of which are even bigger. There's still the same amount of food in the ocean as there was in the pond – you've just got a lot more competition.

No matter what sort of a person you were in high school, now is the time to reassess your beliefs about what it means to be a nerd. In this strange new world of university, nerdiness is your survival tactic. It's time to amp it up to the next level.

Just before you bust out the socks and sandals and bad haircut, though, nerdiness isn't about what you wear, or how thick your glasses are or how few friends you have. Nerdiness is a state of mind. Being nerdy is about knowing what you want and about taking every step you can to ensure that you get it. Nerds are assertive. Nerds are successful. Nerds are sexy.

Arm yourself

Nerdy people don't get special treatment. They face the same pressures as everyone else – fear of failure, unfamiliarity with the academic world and insecurities about themselves. What sets nerdy people apart is their ability to find and use weapons against such pressures. The fact that you're reading this book suggests that you are one of these people.

My story, though, is just that – mine. Everyone who's been to uni has their own and every story is worth hearing. Know someone who's got a degree? Ask them how they did it. Ask them to share their stories of triumph and failure. Their tips and advice are weapons against your unfamiliarity with the academic world. Stock them methodically in your artillery.

Ask your uni for tips. Look out for and sign up to any opportunities for you to build your stockpile. Academic writing skills courses. Learning support centre meetings. Free lectures about effective referencing. Public seminars about cultural awareness on campus. Library tours. Every person's perspective offers a new strategy of attack against the pressures that face all uni students.

Be as assertive as you need to be. Essay writing, academic reading and exam revision are, in a practical sense, completely useless skills. You are not born with this knowledge. It will not help you survive if you get lost in the bush. If you are scared of uni, this probably means that you're a totally normal person who's led a very healthy life up until this point. That fear is fine. You just need to collect enough weapons to shoot it down.

Embrace your stingy side

Another explanation for why people get so nerdy when they reach university is the fact that they are paying for it. People – whether it's students themselves or their families – spend a lot of money to get on campus. Students regularly sacrifice sanitary living conditions and sufficient food just to be able to afford to attend lectures. Parents sacrifice their savings, get second jobs, go without holidays. This mandatory cost sets university apart from high school; although some parents choose to send their children to expensive private schools, this is a choice rather than a necessity. No one should ever have to get into debt in order to go to school in New Zealand.

At uni, though, everyone is in debt. Most students are in debt to the government, many to their parents or other family members, a few to scholarship providers. The debts that don't have to be paid back financially have to be paid back in the form of hard work and results. Funders will expect their fundees to honour their generosity by getting good grades. A gift is not a gift if you expect something in return – it is an investment.

It's not until you recognise that every dollar you're borrowing to be at uni will have to be paid back in some form or another that you can fully embrace your stingy side. It's only then that you can even begin to realise that every 'free' service offered by your uni is actually a very expensive service that your fees go towards helping to pay for. Each course is factored into each dollar you borrow and that you will spend years after your graduation paying back. It's your duty to get your money's worth.

I got a bit carried away with this, taking three essay-writing classes in my first semester. It was totally worth it. Even though a lot of the tips were repeated, I took something new away from every class. Even though my first essays were far from perfect, I got the satisfaction of feeling as if I'd done everything I could to prepare them. Being stingy became part of my ammunition for doing well.

Own the web

Today's uni nerds have to be twenty-first-century nerds. You are expected to be as adept with basic ICT as you are with basic literacy and numeracy. Email is the primary method of communication and you'll need to check your account at least every morning. It only took me one wasted trip (across town, on my bike, in the rain) to an empty lecture theatre to realise that an email about a cancelled lecture is only useful if you read it beforehand.

As well as communication, most information about courses, readings, assessment and enrolment changes is found on your uni's website. It's here that your personal student information will be stored, including your internal transcript – the list of courses you have completed, along with the grade you achieve for each one.

Check your address, courses and emergency contacts. Check to make sure that all your enrolments have been processed properly. If you change a course, this is where you'll come to check that you have been accepted. After exams, this is where you'll come to get your results. This page will convey to you the most important information of your uni career. Get to know it.

Handy link . . . for asking dumb questions about ICT (and just about anything else):

www.dummies.com

Good habit 2: Attend your lectures

All of them. Even the boring ones. Even when you're hung-over. Even when you'd rather be doing something else. An unforeseen crisis, a contagious illness or some life-changing event should be the only real reasons why you should miss a class. I didn't miss a single lecture during my time at uni; I had to leave a couple of them early, but I showed up to every one. I'm not telling you that to brag but so that you can trust me when I tell you that it *is* possible.

It's very easy to skip classes. Most lecturers never take a roll and will post lecture notes and sometimes even video recordings on the internet for those who didn't attend. These are convenient if you're unfortunate enough to be holed up at home with glandular fever for a term. They are no substitute for the real thing.

The real thing, when done well, is magic. Your brain tunes in to what the lecturer is talking about (or at least as much of it as it understands) and then starts to produce its own noise. Ideas pop into your mind in a way they never do when you're viewing the lecture in the computer lab, straining to catch up on every last word that you missed. These ideas, scrawled into the margin of your note sheets, become fodder for your essays. Conversation takes place that never gets included in the lecture summary. Tangents occur, from which you can learn far more than the pre-planned content.

The best thing about lectures, though, is the social aspect. Through the shared acts of showing up to lectures, learning, practising arguments and preparing for exams, you bond with your class. Sounds weird but it's true.

By attending every lecture, I learnt that Emma down the back was terrified of public speaking. I learnt that Matt was always late on a Tuesday because he worked in a rest home until 2.30 p.m. and then had to cycle across town to get to campus. I learnt that Dr Armstrong was a vegetarian. Sarah was the one who always asked 'Are we watching a movie today?' as if we were still in high school. Peter was a mature student who worked at the mechanics' shop across Riccarton Road until he was sixty and then decided he'd go and get a formal education. If given the chance, Richard could talk heatedly about the representation of homosexuality in movies for hours. We all felt moved when Brigid Thompson played songs in her lectures, then embarrassed when they were over.

The more I went to class, the more I wanted to go to class because I wanted to see the people I knew. I wanted to continue that discussion I started with Richard about the defining features of camp cinema. I wanted Brigid Thompson to play another song. I wanted to do well in my essays because maybe Dr Armstrong would refer to my work in a class discussion about something.

If nothing else, remember your inner stinge and go to get your money's worth.

Good habit 3: Learn in lectures

Learning in lectures doesn't come naturally. A healthy adult attention span is about twenty minutes. This may be fine in a great movie – our brains can easily refocus on something that we're finding interesting and we're helped out a lot by how the film's editors have chosen to pace it. In a one-, two- or three-hour lecture, though, where we're on our own and struggling to get our heads around obscure concepts or unfamiliar facts, it's not so useful.

What this means is that in order to learn, you need to try. It won't just happen on its own. Most people in most lectures I attended seemed to think it would and ended up asleep, playing solitaire on their laptops or staring blankly into space. They'd shudder back into life five minutes before the end of class, pack up their things and try to stare down the clock. They'd tap their fingernails on their folders or run a pen nib along an etching on the bench top. They'd whisper amongst themselves. They weren't stupid or spiteful, they were just bored out of their minds.

Don't accept pre-prepared notes

Sometimes your lecturer will post up their PowerPoint slides in advance, allowing you to print them off and save taking your own notes. Don't. Use these notes to help you study later in the term but avoid using them as an alternative to your own. Jotting down your own notes is a great way of keeping your brain focused and active during a lecture. As I got better at learning, I'd write down not only the important information in a lecture but also what I *thought* about this information – the questions that came into my head, my first reactions and my evaluations. Here's an example of some of my notes from PSYC101:

> Wilson and Kelling → Broken Windows Theory 1982 → vandalism/disorder creates more crime. (Study further. Works other way? Unpleasant settings → unpleasant behaviour? Bad coffee → bad mood? WORK INTO ESSAY.)

The first part of this is the raw information – the stuff I'd need to remember for the exams. The second part is my analysis – the questions that came into my head as I processed this information and how I wanted to apply them to my own work. Out of context, they don't make a lot of sense. The evening after I wrote them, though, when I read over them at home, I remembered exactly why I'd written them and was able to develop these scrawled ideas into a more structured argument in my essay.

Reward yourself for learning

It's lame but it works. I'd always have something to eat before a lecture and if I knew it was going to be a tough one, I'd treat myself to a coffee and a muffin from Engineering block. I'd take notes with the new set of rollerball pens I'd bought on sale at the uni bookshop. I might pop a fruit burst in my mouth every twenty minutes to mark the beginning of a new attention span. If it was the last lecture of the day, I'd buy myself a bottle of juice to take in and sip.

Treats reminded me how tough learning in one-, two- or three-hour blocks was and how well I was doing to get through my lectures. No one else will praise you for this so if you want some positive reinforcement, you need to provide it yourself.

Good habit 4: Go to tutorials

Tutorials are as important as lectures. They can be either virtually useless or the making of your degree. How good they are depends on two things: how committed your tutor is and how committed you are. How committed you are depends on how well you assert yourself – something I'll talk more about in 'Good habit 9: Be a somebody'. The commitment of your tutor is entirely beyond your control.

My best tutor engaged me in every tutorial. She overviewed the key points in the lectures and fielded any questions or comments arising from them. She fostered class discussion and helped us to learn through talking and doing rather than reading and writing all the time. She prepared us for our assessment and debriefed with us afterwards. She read my essays – really *read* them – and filled margins with practical, honest suggestions and comments.

She was on hand at all times to answer my questions, respond to my comments and affirm my thinking. She replied to my emails within twenty-four hours. Her passion for the subject area was contagious. She was my personal mentor.

My worst tutor did not prepare for tutorials. She did not read our essays beyond the first page unless she found our writing amusing, in which case she would read them to her flatmates and then relay their comments in class the next day. She gave the impression of not caring one way or the other whether I enjoyed the course or did well in it. Still, her tutorials were worth going to. Whatever kind of tutors you get, you need to go to their tutorials for the following reasons:

1. It'll help your essays. There's every chance that your tutor will mark your essays; even just one essay tip learnt in an hour-long class makes your attendance worth its while.
2. You might get rewarded for it. Many course coordinators ascribe assessment points to tutorial attendance, sometimes allowing you to gain 10 per cent of your entire grade through attendance alone. An hour of tutorial a week is a small price to pay for a boosted overall course mark (the only one that future employers want to know about).
3. You'll do better. If your tutorials are great, you'll walk away feeling as though your questions have been answered; if not, you'll walk away feeling as though they haven't. Either way, you'll be left with a clear sense of what you 'get' and what you don't. You'll know whether you've got adequate support or whether you need to look further. You'll know a lot more about who you are as a student and what you need.
4. You've paid for them. Enough said.

Good habit 5: Read from the beginning

To me as a new student, textbooks were romantic. In my mind, they evoked images of leafy campuses, pretty bohemian people and flirty conversations beside lockers. They'd been a central prop in every teen drama I'd watched during high school; they symbolised maturity, intelligence and independence. As a new uni student, I couldn't wait to get my own.

By the end of my first week on campus, I did. It was a homemade affair – about 25 assorted articles and chapters photocopied then bound together into a thick volume – but I didn't care. Most courses use these compilations – called course readers – because they allow lecturers to pick and choose the readings to fit with the topics they want to focus on. Nowadays, more and more are publishing their course readers online. While this doesn't give you the satisfaction of your own weighty volume, it's much easier to manage.

When I was at uni, all the course readers would come out during the same week and be sold from the same Copy Centre. Those wishing to buy one had to find the correct code on a wall-sized list under the library, fill in an order form and then wait in line. When a student reached the Copy Centre desk he or she would hand the form over to the person on the other side who would then retrieve it, the whole system making it possible to select and purchase without having to speak. If, on reaching the Copy Centre desk, a student did not have the correct form, they would have to start all over again.

The queues of students would snake from one end of the library to the other and then out the front doors and down the main steps into the courtyard or, if it was raining, down the dark internal stairwell into the locker room. To make it to the front of the line, students had two options. The first was to miss their next lecture to wait in line (and then risk the Copy Centre running out of their particular reader anyway). The second was to wait for the lines to drop down to a length that seemed equivalent to the amount of time they had. Keen not to miss a class, I took the latter course of action; it took three days for the line to drop down to a manageable length.

When I finally got to the front of the queue I was met by the Copy Centre administrator, who was boxed in on all sides by colourful stacks of paperwork. Towers of course readers teetered about her, silhouetted like skyscrapers against the light of the window. She smiled grimly as I handed her my order form, pushed her glasses back up her nose and set off into the stacks to search for my request.

In the hope that paying with cash would help to speed up the process, I'd got $20 out of the ATM before I came. As she returned, glasses askew, with my course reader in hand, I thanked her and pushed the note across the desk. She flushed.

'Um, this one's $95, actually.'

I stared.

'We take credit cards.'

After parting with my weekend's wages I cycled home with my course reader. I made myself a strong coffee and a plate of toast with marmalade and sat down outside under the shade of the chestnut tree outside my flat – a suitable setting, I thought, for my first proper foray into academic literature.

I opened the green cover and scanned the contents page. 'The Rise and Fall of Public Broadcasting in New Zealand', '"Global" News Agencies', 'Communication and Cultural

Globalization'. Globalisation! I was practically an expert on this topic now. D. K. Thussu – not a writer I was familiar with, but never mind. I opened the reader to page 95, took a sip of coffee and read:

> The analysis of the effects of the explosion in international communication has been mainly preoccupied with the economic dimensions of globalization at the expense of cultural aspects of interactions between and among the world's people (Carey, 1988; Tomlinson, 1999).

I read it again.

> The analysis of the effects of the explosion in international communication has been mainly preoccupied with the economic dimensions of globalization at the expense of cultural aspects of interactions between and among the world's people (Carey, 1988; Tomlinson, 1999).

Interestingly, this sentence made even less sense the second time. I decided to move on:

> Is globalization another term for Americanization?
> The general pattern of media ownership indicates that the West, led by the USA, dominates the international flow of information and entertainment in all major media sectors. But what is the impact of such one-way flows of global information and entertainment on national and regional media cultures?

I was totally unprepared for these questions. Thussu was the expert and I'd paid a hundred bucks for his expert opinion, not to be asked for mine. How should I know whether globalisation was another term for Americanisation? What *was* Americanisation? 'The West'? An 'international flow' of media? 'All major media sectors'? 'Global information and entertainment'? 'National and regional media cultures'? The more I tried to understand what he was asking me to do, the more I felt convinced that I couldn't do it. Having lost all interest in 'cultural globalization', I read on out of sheer stubbornness.

> It has been argued that international communication and media are leading to the homogenization of culture, but the patterns of global/national/local interactions may be more complex.

During the course of this sentence, a number of droplets had pushed out of the corners of my eyes and blurred my vision. I couldn't see the pages any more. I slammed the course reader against the roots of the chestnut tree and let it slide into a puddle. I'd waited for three days and wasted nearly a hundred bucks and I couldn't even read it. All my life I'd been good at reading but now, when it really mattered, I was useless. I needed to be put in the remedial class. I needed to be kicked out of uni. I threw my toast towards a concerned-looking duck and went inside.

It took me five days to pick the course reader up again. We'd been assigned the first three articles as homework reading and I was behind. Bracing myself for another academic ridiculing, I picked up the reader by its cover and opened it to the first article: 'Understanding the Media' by Eoin Devereux.

> How are we to begin to make sense of the media-saturated world in which most of us live? What sorts of questions

> should we be addressing as students of the twenty-first-century media?

What questions indeed? I liked the fact that Devereux, unlike Thussu, took it as a given that I didn't know this yet. I read on.

> This chapter starts by looking at the main issues that we need to address in order to begin to more fully understand the ever-burgeoning media. We use the Irish rock band U2 and *The Simpsons* television series in order to demonstrate the kinds of questions we can and *should* be raising about the contemporary media. As a key starting point you are encouraged to begin your own intellectual journey through a structured and critical examination of how you personally experience and use the media by means of keeping a media diary.

In one thoughtfully worded introduction, Eoin Devereux saved my self-esteem. He'd used language I could understand and raised the kinds of issues I cared about. By using relative case studies, he had included me in his chapter and, as a result, in my course reader as a whole. I could have kissed him.

After this experience, I always started my course readers at the beginning. Your lecturer – or in the case of a textbook, the author – has thought carefully about the order of these readings. This will reflect not just the order of lecture topics but also the development of your ability to read academic writing, something that doesn't necessarily happen straightaway. There is no point in skipping ahead right at the start.

This experience also taught me that not being able to understand an article does not mean you are not able to understand the ideas in it. It just means that you don't have the skills to translate the language yet. Keep looking up unfamiliar words in dictionaries and, if you're still confused, ask your lecturers to explain them. The more articles you read, the more familiar you'll get with the jargon; you'll know you really get it when you subconsciously start using it yourself.

Good habit 6: *Read* your readings

Motivated by its introduction, I read Devereux's chapter in its entirety. Then I went out for coffee with a friend. I'd gone on a bit about Devereux being a great writer but it wasn't until she asked me what the chapter was about that I realised I didn't actually know. I mumbled something about it being complicated and changed the topic before sculling my coffee and hurrying home. If I was to have Devereux's chapter in my head by tomorrow, I needed to read it again and I needed to read it differently.

When I read it the first time, that's all I did. I read it as I'd read a novel. When I read it the second time, I *read* it. I noted down enough to be able to remember the point of the chapter without having to read the chapter again. I noted it down in a way *I'd* understand and find relevant. I'm sure you already know how to read, but here's how to *read*, and understand it: write down the reference details, take notes, sum up, capture your response – and read even if you hate it.

Write down the reference details

I'd always start by heading a sheet of refill with full reference information from the contents page. Every article you read is potential essay fodder; taking good reference details down now means that you don't have to find and read the article all over again come essay-writing time. I'll show you how to do this properly later on, but just remember to make a note of the following things before and as you read:

- Author's name
- Title of chapter/article
- Title of book/journal or website address
- Year of publication
- Name of publisher
- Place of publisher
- Pages you read
- Pages you got information from

Take notes

As I read through the article again, I noted down what I saw as the key ideas just as I'd do in a lecture – the only difference being that this lecture was written rather than spoken in a lecture theatre. I looked for a good definition of mass media but, failing to find one, wrote instead:

> Media – hard to define. No longer just a case of sender → receiver communication.

After reading Devereux's summary of Denis McQuail's media theory, I wrote:

> Defining the mass media – McQuail (2000) p. 7
> Politically – media allows democratic debate to happen
> – media is a way to exercise power
> Culturally – media defines social norms
> – media provides a shared cultural environment

After reading Devereux's U2 case study, I noted down:

U2 = globalisation

After reading his *The Simpsons* case study, I noted

The Simpsons = globalisation
= a carefully constructed text
= a carrier of messages

Sum up

By this stage I was at the conclusion:

> The twenty-first-century media present the media student with an increasingly complex set of questions. Globalization, technological change and the restructuring of media ownership underscore many of the questions that have been asked about the mass media as well as raising new kinds of issues for all of us in our roles as students and citizens. In this chapter it has been suggested that we need to undertake media analysis in a critical and systematic way. By using a framework that gives equal recognition to the production, content and reception of media texts we can begin to make sense of the increasingly complex media environment in which we live our lives. It is within these parameters that we can now proceed to consider questions – both old and new – about the twenty-first-century media. The overarching theme of this first chapter is that there is much to be gained by considering these questions in a social light.

I used the conclusion to sum up the main points of the chapter:

- Changes in the world (globalisation, technology, who can own media companies) have changed the meaning of 'media'
- To define 'media' we need to look at who makes media products, what's in them and who consumes them in order to get the full picture
- Media's not just technical or political – it's a social mechanism

Capture your response

After summing up the article, I noted down the thoughts floating around my head after reading the chapter:

- 'Understanding Mass Media' as a title is ironic – whole chapter is about how we can't actually understand it
- Re. U2: The band itself is the media product, not the songs they produce?
- What makes a global media product? Why U2?

In a BA, the important thing is not recalling exactly what's in an article but what you thought about it. As soon as you have a thought, you need to write it down and, where possible, talk about it – take it to a class discussion, share it with your lecturer or tutor, debate it with your classmates, flatmates or family. While other people's ideas are currency in the academic world, *your* responses to them are worth just as much and so must be stored meticulously both in your mind and on paper – you will appreciate a good stockpile once it comes time to be assessed on them.

And I was done. I'd compressed 23 pages down to about a page of refill. There were still a few paragraphs that I felt confused about, but the main thing was that I knew roughly what the chapter was about. I could fill someone else in. I'd *read* it.

After Devereux, I used this strategy for every article I read. I kept all my summary pages together in a folder; every time I wrote an essay I'd get this folder out and would check my notes for anything useful. Although it took time to summarise each article properly, it left me with a clear understanding not only of the reading but also what I thought about it. Passively highlighting cool-sounding words did not.

Read, *even if you hate it*

It's okay to hate your readings. When it comes to set readings, hatred is far preferable to ambivalence. Hatred gives you the energy to put together a well-structured critique. Hatred gives you something to talk about. Hatred – by showing you what you disagree with – shows you what you love.

Whether you love or hate your set readings, you have to read them. All of them. Don't believe the people who tell you that you don't need to. Set readings – be they in a course reader, a textbook or, for the more techno-savvy lecturers, an online collection of electronic articles and resources – are the heart of your course. They are the theories and the facts that every lecture is based around. They are very important. They must be read.

It's not just about understanding the content of what you read in your set readings. It's about understanding *how* to read this content, regardless of whether or not you're interested in it. Your readings, if read in the right order, should indicate the level of reading you should be up to – by shunning readings that are too hard, all you're doing is preventing yourself from getting any better. Rather than ditch them, ask your tutor or lecturer for help. Look up summaries of the articles online. Ask your classmates what they thought.

Good habit 7: Read what you want to

As important as your set readings are, the majority of your reading should be chosen by you. As a professional student, it is your job to read all the time. The amazing thing I found out about reading was that the more I did, the more I wanted to do. The more answers I found, the more questions I had. This is the beautiful paradox of research – the more of other people's ideas you take into your head, the more original your own will be.

What's more – it's easy to read what you want. As long as you have internet access, you have the world's biggest library right in your study space. You've got everyone's opinion on every topic. You've got every fact known to humankind. You've got the academic world literally at your fingertips.

Also at your fingertips, though, is every inaccurate, biased and downright filthy idea known to humankind. As a twenty-first-century reader, your hardest job is not finding information but filtering it, letting through the accurate, useful bits and stopping the unhelpful bits before they break through into your real-time life. As a general guide, 'safe' material to incorporate into your uni assignments has:

1. a specified author or authors, or is attributed to a registered group or organisation; and
2. publication details – a publishing company, or formal online publication details.

This doesn't mean you can't read other stuff; it just means you have to be able to identify its limitations and know when to leave it floating in cyberspace rather than weaving it into your university work. When you're reading for interest, all information, however unverified, is useful in its ability to make you *think*. The best academic advice I ever got was from writer Joe Bennett, who put it this way: 'Ideas spring to ideas. Words spring to words. As a writer, you must never underestimate the value of an idea, wherever it comes from.'

I always started with Google. As soon as I'd had an interesting thought – like the one about U2 after the Devereux reading – I'd do a search. I'd read blogs and online magazine articles and budget fan sites about U2. I'd read Wikipedia. Many academics will tell you not to go near Wikipedia with a 10-foot pole. Do not listen to them. Whilst the fact that anyone can contribute to Wikipedia means that it is not a reliable source of factual information (and for this reason should never be referenced in an academic assignment), it is a treasure trove of thinking material.

Reading for inspiration and reading for essay material require different reading approaches. When I read for inspiration, I scanned. I perused this and that. I followed links to other links, not caring whether what I was reading was academically acclaimed or not. At the end of it, I was left with a better sense of how things are and I'd be able to come up with some key ideas and questions. When I read for essay material, I copied. I noted down other people's quotes and ideas, referenced them, then wrote my own responses alongside.

As important as your own reading is, it can't completely override your set reading. One of my first essays asked that I read and incorporate five readings from the course reader into my response. Taking this as a suggestion rather than a rule, I shunned the course reader and focused only on the – in my mind, more interesting – stuff I'd come across from my own reading. This cost my essay a full letter grade. Comments on my essay explained that in proving my research skills I'd neglected to prove that I understood the basic concepts of the course – which were, in essence, what the mark was for.

Read stuff you can touch

As great as Google is, some of the best reading is done off paper rather than a computer screen. Go to the library. Run your hands along the shelves of books. Pick out one that looks pretty and open it up. Hear its spine creak. Smell its dusty pages. Fan them with your thumb. The internet is great but in terms of reading, this is where things get serious.

When you read a book, there are no pop-up ads for Russian brides or gym memberships. There are no enticing emails for performance-enhancing lotions and potions. The content of a book has been reviewed by people other than its author. The book itself has probably been in the library for years, and will still be there in years to come. At a time when ideas can be published in an instant by anyone, anywhere, books have a reassuring permanence.

Some of the most important books in the library are the ones that your lecturer puts on restricted loan. He or she will do this to give as many people as possible the opportunity to read them; while most books can be borrowed for a week or two, restricted loan books can only be borrowed for a few days or, depending on the importance of the book and the number of people in the course, a few hours. The first person to get to the book gets to borrow it first and each student who enquires after them gets put on a waiting list.

While being twentieth in line for a three-hour loan book usually means waiting only a few days, being twentieth in line for a three-day loan book can mean waiting for weeks, often long past the point of the book's being useful to you. This is assuming, as well, that everyone who borrows the book follows the restricted loan rules; while fines start accruing once the time limit has elapsed, I've heard of many students who opt to pay this fine over getting the book back on time. Plus there's the fact that a restricted loan book is just as easy to lose as one that is freely available.

If you want to read a restricted loan book, you should therefore get to the library asap. Run. My first casual walk to the three-hour loan section put me at number 15 on a waiting list. After one week I had progressed to number 12, where I waited for three weeks before a librarian emailed me to say sorry, the girl at number 1 just found the book in the back of her car. That she was fined forty dollars did nothing to change the fact that I wouldn't get to see the book until long after the term had finished.

You can stop running as soon as you've got the sought-after book in your hands. Sit down for a second and look at it. If you only have an hour or so, don't try to read or understand it. Scan the contents page and photocopy the chapters that look the most relevant, keeping an eye on your account balance and the photocopying rules of your university. Photocopy the introduction and the conclusion, as these usually summarise the main points. Always, always, photocopy the title page so that, when the time comes, you have all the necessary reference material at hand.

What I would do at this stage is, using the terrifying automatic staplers any good uni library should have, staple the material from each book in an individual bundle with the title page at the front. Once I'd finish reading through this booklet I'd store it with my other reading material on my study room shelves and use it in future essays. It's amazing how many essay questions one article can be applied and made relevant to.

Sometimes there will be professional sprinters in your class. You can't compete with them. Check to see if other libraries in your area have got the sought-after book. If not, check the bookshops; if you're sneaky about it, you can usually gain enough info from a behind-the-shelves thumb-through without having to pay for it. Another option is searching Google books; depending on its copyright status, you might be able to read enough of the book online to get a feel for its key concepts. If you absolutely can't find the book anywhere, don't stress. Unless your lecturer has said otherwise, you can still get top marks without restricted loan books. A search on the library database computers should reveal plenty of other useful alternatives.

As soon as I'd found some useful books, I'd grab a seat with a view – usually on one of the top floors of the library. Then I'd go straight for the index, where I'd look for words and phrases of interest. Rather than reading the whole book, I'd stick to the chapters that addressed the terms I really wanted to read about.

I'd head up a sheet of refill with the book's reference details and then I'd note down quotes of interest, matching them with a page number in the margin. Photocopying was expensive and lugging books home on my bike was hazardous so – provided I had an hour or so free – I'd copy out what I needed and return the books to the shelves once I was done.

Wherever possible, I'd always try to ask a librarian for help. On a busy day I'd get a library call number scrawled on a Post-it note and a point in the right direction. On a quiet day, I'd get a personal tour of the library and an in-depth assessment of all the books in my line of enquiry. I'd be asked about my degree and my family and my plans for summer. We'd talk about the weather. You just don't get that kind of service from Google.

Good habit 8: Reference everything

You can do all the reading you like but if you don't keep clear records, you won't be able to use any of it in your essays.

Referencing is key to any research assignment. As I've explained, other people's ideas are currency in the academic world. Your job during the semester is not just to read these ideas but also to stockpile and save them so that you can then spend them on your essays or exams. While you can save and spend this academic currency at will, nothing in your ideas bank belongs to you (unless you thought of it yourself) and you cannot spend this currency unless you can attribute it to its rightful owner. This is called referencing.

It's easy to get wrapped up in your readings – and you should – but when you're jotting down the stuff you may want to use later, make sure to jot down the page number as well. If you don't, you're going to face the tedious process of backtracking through a book to find that one killer quote that would fit so perfectly into your essay, if only you could find its source. If you haven't written down the author, title and publishing details, you may not be able to find the book (or journal, or website) at all. No matter how well the quote fits into your essay, including it is not an option if you don't have a reference.

As well as a reference, you have to ensure that the quote is perfectly accurate: the words and punctuation you include within quotation marks or as an indented quote need to be exactly the same as the words in the original publication. Alternatively, you can completely change the quote by putting it into your own words, but you still have to reference the idea to its original author so it's crucial that you get the meaning spot on. So, as you're jotting down quotes and paraphrases from your readings, check them for accuracy. Then double-check them.

In order to reference accurately, the powers that be have developed a number of referencing systems. Each course that you are enrolled in will have adopted one of these systems and, as you need to start stockpiling your academic cash now, it's your job to start referencing everything you read and take notes about as you go. Referencing everything as and when you read it will mean that when you have to write your first essay, you can use the notes you've already taken without having to look up the book or article all over again.

Referencing systems

American Psychological Association (APA)
Often used in: American Studies, Gender Studies, Psychology

Modern Language Association (MLA)
Often used in: English, Philosophy, Cultural Studies

Harvard
Often used in: Mass Communication, Journalism, Sociology, Political Sciences

Oxford
Often used in: History, Classics

How to reference what you cite

There are two main ways to reference what you cite: in-text (APA, MLA, Harvard); and by footnotes or endnotes (Oxford).

In-text references occur, predictably, in the text. Another author's idea can be paraphrased or quoted. If it is paraphrased, the in-text reference is slotted into the sentence to acknowledge and give reference to the source, i.e. the work where you found the idea. There are various ways to do this that are dependent on the referencing system specified by the discipline, the course handbook or the lecturer in charge. If the idea is being quoted, it needs to be included in quotation marks 'like this' (a short quote); or,

> for long quotes (usually three or more lines, or more than 35–40 words), it needs to start on a new line and be indented both sides, a bit like this. In this case it does not need quotation marks.

The in-text reference details – such as the author's name, the date the referenced work was published and the page on which you found the information – must be given in your text. How much detail you need to include, and how you present this detail, depends on the referencing style you are using. Brief examples are given below, but remember that there are more complex citations than these, for instance multiple-author works. Always check your course outline or ask your lecturer which style to use.

APA

Paraphrase of general idea:

Referencing is a central aspect of a research essay (Jury, 2012).

OR

Jury (2012) argues that referencing is a key part of a research essay.

Short introduced direct quote:

Jury (2012) argues that '[r]eferencing is key to any research assignment' (p. 72).

Short direct quote:

'Referencing is key to any research assignment' (Jury, 2012, p. 72).

Long quote:

Long indented quotes can be referenced in one of two main ways. If the quote is introduced by referring to the author (with the year of publication following in brackets), then at the close of punctuation at the end of the quote, only the page number (or numbers) needs to be given in brackets. If the source is not used to introduce the quote, then the author, year of publication and page number(s) will appear after the final punctuation mark in brackets. The second type of citation would look like this. (Jury, 2012, p. 72)

MLA

Paraphrase of general idea:

Referencing is a central aspect of a research essay (Jury 72).

OR

Jury argues that referencing is a key part of a research essay (72).

Short introduced direct quote:

Jury argues that '[r]eferencing is key to any research assignment' (72).

Short direct quote:

'Referencing is key to any research assignment' (Jury 72).

Long quote:

Use the same format as for APA, but without the date and without p. or pp. – just cite the author's surname (if not used to introduce the quote) and/or the page number(s) in brackets after the concluding punctuation of the quote. (Jury, 72)

Harvard

Paraphrase of general idea:

Referencing is a central aspect of a research essay (Jury 2012).

OR

Jury (2012) argues that referencing is a central aspect of a research essay.

Short introduced direct quote:

Jury (2012, p. 72) argues that '[r]eferencing is key to any research assignment'.

OR

Jury (2012: 72) argues that '[r]eferencing is key to any research assignment'.

Short direct quote:

'Referencing is key to any research assignment' (Jury 2012, p. 72).

OR

'Referencing is key to any research assignment' (Jury 2012: 72).

Long quote:

As for APA, but with no comma between author's name and year of publication. (Jury 2012, p. 72)

Oxford

Whereas the other styles incorporate the reference details into the text, either within sentences or, in the case of long quotations, at the end of the quote and outside its final punctuation, the Oxford style incorporates a small superscript number.[1] This corresponds with a number either at the bottom of the page (a footnote) or at the end of your essay (endnote). The bonus of this system is that it's less intrusive and doesn't cut into your word count so much.

The first time you reference an author's work, you need to include its full reference in the footnote or endnote. From then on, if you refer to that work, you can use a short reference like this.[2]

Full references

Full references contain the full information about your sources. Whereas in-text and citation references show your readers which ideas are yours and which are others', full references allow your readers to look up the sources you have read themselves.

The final page of your essay is your reference list, a separate page on which you list the full references in alphabetical order for every source you have referred to in your essay.

The following examples are partly fanciful, just to illustrate the various referencing styles. It should also be noted that there are many websites that give examples of these styles, and that there are inconsistencies and differences between them. Use the guide your course or university supplies and follow that. The principles stay the same, but the details of punctuation, use of upper and lower case etc., vary.

1 Rebecca Jury, *BA: An Insider's Guide*, Auckland University Press, Auckland, 2012, p. 77.

2 Jury, p. 77. Actually, for notes like this one which directly repeat the previous reference, instead of a short reference you can use 'ibid.' – it's short for the Latin word *ibidem*, meaning 'in the same place'.

APA

Whole book:

Jury, R. (2012). *BA: An insider's guide*. Auckland, New Zealand: Auckland University Press.

Chapter in a book:

Jury, R. (2012). Get Good Habits. In R. Jury (Ed.), *BA: An insider's guide* (pp. 41–84). Auckland, New Zealand: Auckland University Press.

Article in a journal:

Jury, R. (2012). Get Good Habits. *Journal of Study Skills, 38*(4), 40–50.

Online source:

Jury, R. *BA: An insider's guide blog*. Retrieved January 28, 2012, from www.aninsidersguide.com.

MLA

Whole book:

Jury, Rebecca. *BA: An Insider's Guide*. Auckland: Auckland University Press, 2012.

Chapter in a book:

Jury, Rebecca. "Get Good Habits." *BA: An Insider's Guide*. Ed. Rebecca Jury. Auckland: Auckland University Press, 2012. 41–84.

Article in a journal:

Jury, Rebecca. "Get Good Habits." *Journal of Study Skills* 38.4 (2012): 40–50.

Online source:

Jury, Rebecca. "BA: An Insider's Guide Blog." 28 January 2012. <www.aninsidersguide.com>.

Harvard

Whole book:

Jury, R. 2012. *BA: an insider's guide*. Auckland: Auckland University Press.

Chapter in a book:

Jury, R. 2012. Get Good Habits, in R. Jury, ed., *BA: an insider's guide*. Auckland: Auckland University Press: 41–84.

Article in a journal:

Jury, R. 2012. Essays. *Journal of Study Skills*, 38(4): 40–50.

Online source:

Jury, R. 2012. *BA: an insider's guide blog*. [Online]. Available from: http://www.aninsidersguide.com [28 January, 2012].

Oxford

The full references in your reference list are similar to those that appeared in your footnotes or endnotes when you referenced a source in your essay for the first time.

Whole book:

Jury, R., *BA: An Insider's Guide*. Auckland University Press, Auckland, 2012.

Chapter in a book:

Jury, R., 'Get Good Habits', *BA: An Insider's Guide*, R. Jury (ed.), Auckland University Press, Auckland, pp. 41–84.

Article in a journal:

Jury, R., 'Essays'. *Journal of Study Skills*, vol. 38, no. 4, 2012, pp. 40–50.

Online source:

Jury, R., 'Essays', *Journal of Study Skills*, vol. 38, no. 4, 2012, pp. 40–50, viewed on 28 January 2012, <http://www.aninsidersguide.com>.

Good habit 9: Be a somebody

I started uni, like everyone else, as a nobody. It's not that I really *was* a nobody, it's just that uni was a scary new environment in which I hadn't yet got into the habit of expressing myself as an individual. As I struggled to get to grips with the way my new world worked, I conveyed very little of myself and so my lecturers and classmates knew very little of me. I behaved like everyone else and, as a result, blended seamlessly into the student masses.

I wore jeans and jandals and carried a brown leather satchel over my shoulder. I took notes with a navy Biro on lined refill or, on wet days when I took the bus rather than my bike, typed notes into a silver laptop. I stared at the lecturer until he or she took off his or her glasses and asked the class 'What do you think?', at which time I stared at my notes, hoping the answer would reveal itself to me.

I became a somebody at uni one wet afternoon in a COMS tutorial. It was essay-returning day and, poised behind a three-foot stack of essays, our tutor was telling us what we'd done wrong.

'Not enough references,' she was saying, jabbing the top of the stack with the lid of her whiteboard marker. 'Donald likes at least six references.'

A guy raised his hand. 'But the question said we only needed five.'

The tutor rolled her eyes and jabbed the pile again. 'You only *need* five. But *Donald* likes six.'

Donald? The guy with the paisley shirt and the PowerPoint who gives the lectures? Dr Matheson? *He* read my essay? Until that point I hadn't really considered the fact that *somebody* would actually pick up my piece of writing, read it through and develop an opinion about it. Now that I thought about it, though, those question marks and ticks down the margin and that letter-in-a-circle at the end must have been put there by somebody. Somebody with likes and dislikes, irrational hates and favourite words, somebody who gets bored and excited and inspired.

For some reason – be it his position at the front of the lecture theatre, his shirts or his title – I hadn't really thought of Dr Matheson as a real person, as someone I could engage and connect with. I knew he was smart and important – but I just didn't really think about him as having a soul.

Lecturers have souls too

The sooner you realise that your lecturer has a soul, the sooner you can start writing for a real person. The sooner you see the reality of this, the sooner you can start to find your own feet and, even more importantly in this strange new city, your own voice. It's natural to respect your lecturer's intellect and experience and to feel a little intimidated by his or her higher education. These things make them smart and authoritative. They do not make them gods. While most lecturers have PhDs, they also have families, friends, interests, hobbies, insecurities and unhealthy obsessions. Other than the letters after their names, they are people just like you.

As soon as I saw Dr Matheson as a person – Donald – and, more importantly, the person who would be reading my essays, I started enjoying uni a whole lot more. Where simply voicing my opinion in class seemed pointless, posing a question to a real person at the front of the classroom was fun and interesting. Where writing for a question seemed like a pointless exercise, writing for a person was a challenge.

My next essay was planned with Donald in mind. Would I try to win him over by supporting the theorists he preached about in lectures? Or could I surprise him by challenging these theorists' work? Might I attempt to appeal to his ego by referencing his own journal articles? Or would I try to engage him by incorporating a host of new, obscure theorists into my work?

I tried all of these approaches in all of my courses. The essays I wrote for a particular person were enjoyable to write, got better grades, and gave my lecturers and I something to talk about. Through these essays, I became a somebody myself.

Respect your boss

Yes, they have souls but if your degree is your job, your lecturers are your employers. While you can be friendly, you shouldn't be friends with the person who needs to remain objective about marking your work. I often used email to run ideas back and forth about an essay with a lecturer but I wouldn't email them an account of my weekend (and certainly no photos of a messy night out). I'd use their office hours to go over essay plans but I wouldn't ask them to meet me at The Foundry for a beer. If they used it to introduce themselves, I'd call them by their first name – Dr Donald Matheson, for example, I called 'Dr Matheson' at the start and then 'Donald' once I'd got to know him a bit better.

Getting these kinds of relationships right can be a fine balance so it's generally safest to follow your lecturer's lead. Their replying to your emails straightaway, inviting you to their office for a chat about the course or signing their emails with 'best' or 'warm regards' are good signs that you've got it right. Their ignoring your emails, avoiding you on campus or telling you to let other students have a turn to talk are pretty clear signals that you might want to ease off a bit.

Keep cool

While asserting yourself is an important part of being a somebody, over-asserting yourself can lead to your being the sort of somebody who gets on everyone's nerves. In my experience, there's always one person in each class who falls into this category: John from first-year psychology who would say things like 'But doesn't that just contradict hundreds of years of sociological inquiry?' every time the lecturer introduced a new theorist; Rachel in cultural studies who compared every author to Salman Rushdie; Jason in COMS who just wouldn't shut up about 'the power of the mass media' – we knew them all and we hated them all and, from our lecturers' pained expressions every time one of them cleared their throat to speak, it was clear that they did too.

Wary of inspiring this hatred but needing to be known, I set myself the goal of contributing one point to every in-class discussion – not every lecture, just every time I could see that my lecturer was trying to foster some conversation. I might pipe up with 'Yes!' when the class was asked whether they felt that Jane Eyre was driven by sex. I might wait until the last ten minutes of the lecture – which I knew the lecturer set aside for questions – to ask how exactly Baudrillard defined 'simulacrum'. Speaking up once in a class discussion was an achievable goal for me and meant that I could walk away feeling as if I'd made a decent contribution. Having said something made me feel as if I was part of it all, as if I'd become somebody to my peers and lecturers and, in doing so, the whole thing became more worthwhile.

Set a goal that is achievable for you and appropriate to the situation, and work to meet it. If you're a shy person, speaking up once in every fourth or fifth discussion might be more do-able than every time. If you feel like piping up every time anyone else says anything, sticking to two or three comments per discussion might be more appropriate. Generally, though, unless your lecturer or tutor asks a question, it's best to keep quiet. Save your questions until the end of the lecture and let the lecturer get on with delivering the content that everyone in the class has paid to hear. And save at least some of your thoughts and questions for your tutorials, that rely on and encourage more participation than lectures generally do.

Good habit 10: Don't do your uni work all the time

If you're going to enjoy your uni work, you have to enjoy other things as well. As humans, we're sociable beings who need a range of things going on in our lives to stay happy. Doing nothing but study while you're at uni will likely make you resent the very material you're there to enjoy and will quickly drive you mad.

Step 6
Make it fun

While getting a degree is an amazing thing to do, uni's an amazing place to be and you're missing a lot if you don't take the time to soak up the vibe of the place. Yes, it's a city but it's a city unlike any other you'll find in the world. It's a place where difference is celebrated, where risk-taking is expected, where everyone's so used to asking questions that things are constantly being rethought, revamped and reconsidered.

Central to this environment is the uni magazine. Generally produced each week, it's a varied mix of journalistic articles on current issues in your area, advertising, silly stuff and letters. Whether you enjoy the writing or not, if you want to be able to take part in on-campus gossip, you pretty much have to read the magazine. While I was at uni, some of the debates between the editor and anonymous students on the letters page of *Canta*, the weekly publication of the University of Canterbury Students' Association, went on for months; everyone would become a suspect as the whole uni scouted for clues of the scandalous letter writer's identity.

Another fun thing about uni is the random exhibits. As a site of major academic research, universities are likely to house all sorts of amazing artifacts that come and go from foyers and lobbies throughout the year. During my time at uni, tables of ancient pottery would appear and disappear from the library in the course of a week. Mannequins in full ethnic costume would take residence in stairwells without warning. Once, the entire ground floor of one library was occupied with a collection of alternative footwear designs.

Then there are the archives. Canterbury's James Hight Library has newspaper records spanning back for decades. Behind the three-hour loan section is a little room housing microfiche and microfilm viewers – devices into which you can feed film and slides, full of super-compacted words and images – and view them through a magnifier on a screen. The Macmillan Brown Library houses a near-complete set of trial documents belonging to one of the judges from the Tokyo War Crimes trial, widely regarded as one of the most significant trials of the twentieth century. Most of these archives can be found online, but so what? The experience of trawling through the real documents allows you to *feel* history in the flesh and that's an unbeatable experience.

Artifacts aside, so much of a university's history and character are set into its buildings and grounds. Explore. Where earlier you explored to find your way around, this time explore to enjoy the place. Stroll through the sports fields. Ask if there's a marae or fale on campus and, if so, go and have a look; these can be some of the most vibrant places on campus. Check out the architecture and think about what it says about the era in which the university was built. Think about all the students who've gone before you. Wander over to the ruckus in the quad and check out whatever competition or debate or demonstration is on today.

Review the cafés. There should be a good mix, with some that appeal to you more than others. Take note of prices before writing off a packed lunch as something your mum made you at primary school, though. The development of students' associations from support services into businesses run by enterprising young marketing students has resulted in the demise of the cheap on-campus student feed. When I started uni, the price of a cheese scone was around $1.20. By the time I was finishing, two years later, it had more than doubled. When I left uni, most things in campus cafés were the same price that I'd pay in an inner-city café.

When you're on a budget, it's about finding the food items with the best filling-to-cost ratio. Scones, muffins, scrolls and bread rolls are usually the winners. On campus, carbs are your friend; make up for any dietary deficiencies at home by stocking up on cheap sources of protein, getting plenty of calcium, and eating heaps of fresh fruit and veges.

Eating and drinking like a student isn't about going without, it's about identifying what you want, then finding a cheaper alternative – sure, you could pay $4 for a flat white, or you *could* pay $1 for a black filter coffee and then use as much free milk as you want (often it gets even cheaper if you bring your own mug). Yes, the branded water bottles are cool but at $3.50 a pop you could just buy one and then refill it from one of the water fountains scattered around campus. Sure, you could buy a scone from uni for $2.50, or you *could* buy a pack of six from the supermarket down the road for $5.

Spend at least one night at the student bar. Whether you choose to go back again is up to you, but it is an integral part of the student experience and holds vast potential for fun on campus. If you're not a drinker it's just as much fun to go and watch everyone else getting sloshed. No one gets drunk quite like a uni student.

Find your niche

As fun as this new city is, it's still huge and it's important to find your place within it. Although it may at first seem as if there's only one culture at uni – the culture of academia – the longer you stay the easier it is to see that it's actually made up of a whole heap of subcultures, all bound together by their common academic goals.

Just like at school, uni students naturally fall into different groups. The difference is that while different groups tend to stand apart at school, at uni there's enough space for them all to get along without getting in each other's faces. Your uni's celebration of cultural diversity – whether that's based on iwi or whanau, where you're from, what you enjoy doing or who you love – is embodied in the dozens of support and interest groups you can access there.

All you need to do is seek them out. At any time, your university's students' association – identifiable by the SA in their initials (UCSA for University of Canterbury Students' Association, AUSA for Auckland University Students' Association and so forth) – is on hand to provide you with information, support and contacts, so pop in and pay them a visit.

Always remember: you're never just a student. You're a social, cultural being with a totally unique background and experience, so seek out the support at uni that caters for you. Meeting like-minded people can be a good way to start you off, especially if you're new to town, but mixing with new sorts of people is one of the fun things about being at uni. So, use the support groups as a base, then branch out as you get more comfortable with your new environment. A quick search on your uni's website will lead you quickly to contacts for the support services and interest groups that are relevant to you. Otherwise, jump on to your students' association website to see what they can offer. Whatever sort of student you are – Maori, Pasifika, international, mature, straight from school, the first in your family to go to university, gay, in a wheelchair, at uni on a scholarship – enter it into the search tool and follow the links to the contacts and services that cater for you.

Handy links . . . for students' associations across New Zealand:

Auckland University of Technology Student Movement
www.ausm.org.nz

The Auckland University Students' Association
www.ausa.auckland.ac.nz

Lincoln University Students' Association
www.lusa.org.nz

Massey University Students' Association
www.musa.org.nz

University of Canterbury Students' Association
www.ucsa.org.nz

Otago University Students' Association
www.ousa.org.nz

University of Waikato Students' Union
www.wsu.org.nz

Victoria University of Wellington Students' Association
www.vuwsa.org.nz

Clubs

Clubs are a uni staple – there's likely to be over a hundred operating on your campus. Join one. Get on to your uni's students' association website and browse the range of clubs on offer until you find something you like the look of.

One of the great things about uni clubs is that if you can't find what you're looking for, you can make your own. Banners made out of sheets, chalk messages on footpaths, posters on noticeboards, ads in the students' magazine – on campus, it's all fair game in the name of attracting fellow club members. In this city of thousands, there's bound to be at least a couple of other people who think that your club's a good idea.

Not convinced? Here's a taster of some of the uni clubs on offer around New Zealand:

The University of Auckland:
Dessert Club
Drinking Club
PokeClub (Pokemon-based social network)

University of Canterbury:
AnimeSoc
SEAL (the Super Exciting And Lovable club)
SAGA Incorporated (Dungeons and Dragons and wargaming)

University of Otago:
Roleplaying Society
Fire Performance and Juggling Club
St Kessog Club (historical re-enactments of pre-seventeenth-century European and Asian history)

Politics

Universities have always been political places. From what I can tell, there are three main reasons for this. Firstly, most people learn a lot about the world and its injustices while they're at uni, and in doing so get passionate these issues. Secondly, after a few rounds of essays, arguing is second nature to most students.

Thirdly, uni in New Zealand is a liberal place in which most well-argued cases are, if not agreed with, accepted.

There is a lot of voting. As a student, I seemed to be forever posting slips into boxes – whether it was my vote for a new students' association president, my thoughts on a proposed new recycling system or my feelings towards a new change to the student loan scheme. Opting in to your uni's students' association gives you more opportunities to have your say over the way your uni is run. It's your choice whether you want to be involved; involvement can be anything from casting a vote to sitting for the student executive.

As important as democracy is on campus, some issues just can't be resolved with a vote. Sometimes issues are bigger than what a petition can tackle. Sometimes it's better to express your opinion by *doing* rather than saying. Sometimes, just sometimes, you need to protest.

As a student I attended a civil-rights-style sit-in in one of the main lecture theatres on campus. We'd just heard that the Vice-Chancellor was in the process of culling some of the less-popular subjects in order to save on the cost of paying the teaching staff in those areas. To your average citizen, this might sound like a logical idea – save money by cutting costs. To a uni student, this was an outrage. Who was the Vice-Chancellor to decide which knowledge could be passed on to new generations of students? Who's to say that just because a course isn't popular, it isn't worthwhile? What kind of a democratic country do we live in? This was mind control of the highest order!

So we sat in. A group of students and lecturers occupied A1 lecture theatre until people noticed. It took days, not that anyone was watching the clock. There were lectures and movies and speeches about the costs of capitalism. Yes, the Vice-Chancellor's decision made practical sense but the *principle* of the matter required immediate action. As a student, nobody should care quite as much about the principle of the matter as you do.

Silly stuff on campus

Stuff happens at uni that wouldn't happen in the real world. Silly stuff. Why? Uni students are not average New Zealand citizens – they are, as I've discussed, nerdier than average people with a lot of time on their hands and, often, not enough maturity to use it constructively. This leads to silly stuff of the highest calibre.

To keep their minds active during long study sessions in the law library, Blake and his best friend Ryan would create treasure hunts. Being students' treasure hunts, there was never any treasure. It wasn't about prizes. It was just silly stuff to give two smart guys a break from study, while still keeping them in the library.

One morning, for example, Blake handed Ryan a piece of paper with 'Wigmore Falls' written on it (the name of a waterfall in Rarotonga that Blake had visited over the summer). After some online research and an exploration of the library, Ryan made the connection to John Henry Wigmore, a legal expert who had written a series of encyclopeadic volumes on the law of evidence.

He searched for a physical link to John Henry Wigmore on campus and, on the library database, located the *Wigmore on Evidence* volumes in the law library. Once in front of them, he looked for another sign – one book of the volume placed incorrectly on the shelf below – and opened the front cover. Inside was the next clue.

During their time at uni, Blake and Ryan's clues went from challenging to fiendish. What started as a way of fighting boredom became a battle of wits. The librarians got used to seeing one or the other repositioning furniture, scaling bookshelves and leaning over balconies in the name of 'research'.

One afternoon Blake received a pxt of an air vent from Ryan, without any description or explanation. After a search of the law library, Blake discovered that air vents of the same variety had been installed in the second floor. Phone in one hand, he proceeded to check every vent until he found one that matched the pxt. As other students abandoned their textbooks to watch, Blake calmly stood on a table to remove the vent cover, extracted the scrap of paper Ryan had left there, replaced the cover and strolled off in search of the next clue.

Blake's best clue was never solved. The first part of the hunt was fairly standard – five typically obscure clues leading Ryan to five typically obscure books on the third floor. Inside the fifth book, though, was an ambiguous reference to tunnel vision. Ryan was stumped. Hopelessly confused, he pulled out the five books in the hope of finding some common link between them. Then he saw. The spaces the books had left in the shelves had created a tunnel of vision, at the end of which lay the book in which the next clue was hidden.

This clue read: 'Lying under canvas, like a man lay dead by the marsh.' Ryan found every legal book he could find by authors called Marsh. He fanned their pages for clues. He checked their spines, inside their cover jackets, in the old issuing pocket at the back. He found a painting of a marsh in amongst the landscapes and looked behind, above and around it. With only a couple of weeks left on campus, Blake kept quiet and waited.

Blake told me this story on our way to uni for his graduation morning tea. En route to the venue, he pulled me into the law library and led me to the third floor. He stopped in front of a large portrait of a lady. I read the plaque. Dame Ngaio Marsh. Famed crime writer. First book: *A Man Lay Dead*. Smiling, Blake pointed to a tiny scrap of paper peeking out from behind the frame, just beside Dame Ngaio's left ear. For all I know, it's there to this day.

Jobs

If you've got time to spend on silly stuff, you could consider getting a job. For me, a casual administration position helped develop my skills and pay for my living expenses while I was studying. Others rely on loans and caregiver generosity for this. These people have more time to concentrate on their studies, making them – in theory – more likely to finish assignments on time and study thoroughly for their exams.

In practice, I haven't found this to be true. The people I've known with manageable commitments outside of uni are much more time-conscious, meaning that any free time they have is highly valued and used efficiently. In contrast, the people I've known with all the time in the world are generally the least effective in their studies; time is like any other commodity – hard to value and measure when you have a limitless supply of it.

While your lecturers will try to talk you out of a job, in my experience the old cliché of 'if you want something done, ask a busy person' is almost always accurate. My advice would be to keep yourself busy enough to value the study time you do have but not busy enough that you feel in any way rushed or pressured with your uni work. Your degree *is* a job, remember, and it's the only one you're paying to do.

Handy link . . . for finding student-friendly jobs:

Student Job Search
www.sjs.co.nz

Volunteering

Another option if you've got free time is volunteer work. I started volunteering at Youthline two weeks before my courses began and worked a three-hour shift there every week for the rest of my degree. I loved my work the most when exams were looming or when I'd just got negative feedback on an essay – working as a counsellor during these times helped me to put my uni life in perspective and, in doing so, get a clearer picture of what I needed to do to perform at my best. What's more, working with other counsellors meant that I always had an empathetic, supportive social network where I could vent my frustrations and be inspired by other people's stories.

At times during my degree I would become disillusioned with the academic world. I'd spend hours tying my brain in knots over the futility of essays, references and theorists. My volunteer work provided balance during these times and helped me to feel as if I was making a difference – as if the brain inside my head was contributing something to society rather than spinning out another well-structured argument about something theoretical and vague.

Practically speaking, volunteering enabled me to develop the skills and experiences that employers go mad for. It looks great on my CV, both for the skills I developed in my role and the fact that I was able to manage my time well enough to do it at all. Take it from me, though – being able to manage a time commitment to volunteering isn't enough. You need a lot of self-motivation, resilience and passion about your volunteer work if you're going to take it on alongside uni and paid work and not see your performance suffer in any of the three. As I said before, 'student' is your main occupation so anything else you do needs to work around that.

Handy link . . . for an up-to-date list of volunteer positions available across New Zealand:

www.volunteernow.org.nz

Step 7
Master the essay

I first came across the word 'essay' somewhere in the early years of high school and, just as I do with most words I am scared of, I gave it a personality. From that moment, every time I heard the word 'essay' I saw an old, grey-bearded scholar sitting at an oak desk surrounded by stacks of curling paperwork. He wore round spectacles and a heavy brown cape and wrote furiously with a quill about things I didn't understand. I imagined that if I spoke to him, he would ignore me; that if he spoke to me, I wouldn't understand him. He knew everything but could relate to nothing. He was full of knowledge but completely detached from reality.

This little old fuddy-duddy stayed in my head throughout my high school years. At that time in my life, 'Essay' signified a culture wholly detached from mine: a culture of rules, regulations and intellectual snobbery, a culture personified by the grey-bearded scholar. In essay-based exams, I stumbled blindly between paragraphs without any clear idea of where I was going or how I'd get there. My markers would scrawl words like 'unsubstantiated', 'undeveloped' and 'relevance?' in my margins, words that meant nothing to me.

In Year 13 I changed to a school that allowed students to choose their own assessments. I took English but managed to avoid writing a single essay all year. I closed the door on the old fuddy-duddy and left him to his scholarly ramblings while I strode through poetry folios and journalistic assessments. He faded into the background of my life, joining the other regrettable memories of my adolescence.

I got my first essay assignment on my first day of uni. By the end of my first week, I had four. I scanned the questions, seeing only the indecipherable ramblings of my bespectacled fuddy-duddy. Although I'd always felt sure that I knew what the purpose of essay writing was – to show the marker how well one could write like a grey-bearded scholar – I'd managed to avoid essays so well to this point that I still had no idea how to do this. I read some pieces by noted academics and tried to copy their style.

Once I thought I'd got this right, I sat down and wrote my answer to the question in one blind sweep, leaving a blank line between my meanderings whenever I remembered to. I checked it over, added in a few more adjectives and replaced some boring, everyday words with fancy-sounding ones from the Microsoft thesaurus.

My first essay return was devastating. Every adjective I'd added had been slashed out with a red rollerball. Every sentence I'd so carefully constructed using only the most academic-sounding language had a large question mark in its margin with the word 'UNCLEAR' scratched alongside in caps. Every fancy word I'd found in the thesaurus had been overwritten with my original, boring, *dumb-sounding* choice. At the end of the essay were a series of bullet points that listed things like 'lack of clarity', 'muddled structure', 'flowery language' and 'ideas clouded by wordiness'.

I'd got it wrong. Essays weren't bearded old scholars with glasses. With no experience to go on, I'd let myself be guided by my own interpretation of the word 'essay' and my own fear of rejection from the academic world. My first essay wasn't an argument; it was a desperate plea for acceptance into a culture I'd constructed in my own head.

The fuddy-duddy had to go. For my next assignment, I told myself that I was writing a structured response with evidence.

No essay about it. I wrote in my own words and stuck to the simplest language I could find. I started getting someone else to read it and comment on how clear it was before I handed it in. In time, my language naturally become more sophisticated and I started using 'academic' words without realising that I was doing so. Regardless of your writing level, you need to write using the simplest language *you* know, not the language you've seen others using, or the language you imagine a 'clever' essay might contain.

Make time

Essay writing is a process. It has three major stages: researching, writing and structuring. Soon into my uni career I worked out that each of these stages, if done properly, takes about a week. Think about it: if essays were meant to be written in a night, why do lecturers almost always hand the assignments out three weeks before the due date? It's not because they want you to choose one night within that three-week period to get the job done. It's because they know that good essays aren't written but crafted, and just like any other feat of craftsmanship – whether it's cheese, wine or boot making – essay making takes time.

Committing yourself to spending time on your essays is not enough. You need to set that time aside and plan how you'll use it. You need to commit not just to spending time on essay writing but also to *not* spending time on something that's more fun. You need to schedule in time to write your essay but also to devote yourself to crafting your essay. As soon as

I got the details of an essay assignment, I'd write them on the calendar:

Friday 16 March
ENGL102 essay due
5 p.m.
1500 words. 25%

To remind myself that essay writing is a process of craftsmanship, I'd write in the one- and two-week-to-go dates as well.

Friday 2 March
ENGL102 essay
due in
TWO WEEKS

Friday 9 March
ENGL102 essay
due in
ONE WEEK

I'd try to keep the calendar as free as possible over the two weeks before my essay was due. I'd make sure that nothing else would make it to the calendar on the two days before. If I was to produce a fully formed essay, I needed to give the essay-writing process time to develop. Essays didn't control my life – I controlled my life around my essays.

Choose the most interesting question

To write well, you have to be interested. When you're interested in your essay topic the research is a pleasure rather than a necessity. Your writing will flow without having to be forced out. Ideas, as Joe Bennett said, will lead to ideas. You will enjoy writing your essay and, as a result, your marker will enjoy reading it. When you truly enjoy writing an essay, whether or not you get a high mark for it isn't so important to you and, because of this, it's much more likely that you will.

Once you've picked the most interesting-looking question, read it. Read it again. Is it a discuss, explain or outline question? Is it asking you to compare or contrast? Explore, argue or debate? Is it asking you to do something that you don't know how to do, like 'explicate', 'delineate' or 'postulate'?

It's crucial first that you find out what all these terms mean. For example, to compare is to look for similarities, not differences. So if you're asked to compare, don't contrast. And if you're asked to compare and/or contrast, don't focus on only one entity or idea. Be clear about how exploring something is likely to be more discursive than arguing or debating something.

When I took SOCI111 in 2007, it was a very popular course with a number of lecturers who would run different lectures based on their areas of expertise. The following questions relate to four of the topics we looked at as a class before being given this assignment: sexualities, family, death and dying, and gambling. They represent a good cross-section of the style of questions you may be asked in any Arts course.

Question 1: Critically discuss and compare research by two sociologists, or other social scientists, that attempts to illustrate the ways in which sexuality is 'socially constructed'.

Key instructive words:

> **Critically**. To look at something critically is to look at both the strengths and limitations, assessing both and then drawing some kind of conclusion from them.
>
> **Discuss**. To discuss is to look at an issue – usually one that is up for debate – and analyse it closely from a range of perspectives, giving a thorough overview of the associated issues.
>
> **Compare.** To compare is to hold two or more things up together and look for the similarities between them.

This essay is asking you to do the following:

1. research two sociologists/social scientists who have focused on sexuality as 'socially constructed';
2. study their findings closely;
3. explain each set of findings carefully, exploring the strengths and limitations and the different perspectives from which they could be seen;
4. draw similarities between the two sets of findings.

You'd need to be careful not to:

- focus too much on the negatives – being critical isn't just about being negative;
- analyse one particular part of the research rather than discuss it in its entirety;

- contrast rather than compare – as mentioned above, to compare is to look for similarities, not differences.

Question 2: What is a family? What problems arise when we try to define the concept in contemporary New Zealand society?

Key instructive words:

> **What.** To answer the question 'what', you need to give a clear definition, which you reach after explaining and assessing a range of possibilities.
>
> Other than 'what', there are none! This is a tricky question, because it gives you no instruction as to how to answer the question – there are no verb instructions for you to follow. I chose this question in 2007 on the basis that I was interested in the topic, and only realised after I'd completed all my research how tricky it was going to be to answer it. Whereas at first I didn't understand the focus of this essay, with the benefit of hindsight, I can see that it's a 'describe and discuss' question. Your marker will be looking for you being able to figure this out.

This essay is asking you to do the following:

1. describe what a family is;
2. discuss the issues around doing so in the twenty-first century.

You'd need to be careful not to:

- spend too much time describing what a family is, and not enough on discussing the implications;
- use one definition of family, without properly exploring others;

- plough ahead with your discussion without having properly defined the key term of family.

Question 3: Why is death and dying such an important topic for sociology? Illustrate with New Zealand examples.

Key instructive words:

> **Why.** To answer the question 'why', you need to give a thoughtful, broad but relevant account of the question being asked. So, where a 'what' question asks for a reasoned, researched definition, a 'why' question asks for an assessment, backed up with evidence.
>
> **Illustrate.** To illustrate is to explain your answer by referring to evidence.

This essay is asking you to do the following:

1. find examples that show the significance of death and dying as a sociology topic in New Zealand;
2. explain why death and dying is a significant sociological topic;
3. use the examples you have found to back up your answer.

You'd need to be careful not to:

- get so tied up in your examples that you don't answer the question clearly;
- get so tied up in answering the questions that your examples are an afterthought;
- stray away from the New Zealand context.

Question 4: Critically assess the view that gambling has been normalised in New Zealand society. In your response, you may like to draw on one type of gambling as an example.

Key instructive words:

Critically. To look at something critically is to look at both the strengths and limitations, assessing both and then drawing some kind of conclusion from them.

Assess. To assess a view is to explain the pros and cons of this view before coming to a conclusion about it.

Draw on. To draw on an example is to focus on it and to use elements of it to support your argument.

This essay is asking you to do the following:

1. explain what you feel are the strengths and limitations of the view that gambling has been normalised in New Zealand society – what is accurate and innaccurate about this statement;
2. show that you know what 'normalised' means;
3. come to some kind of conclusion about the validity of this view;
4. structure your assessment around one type of gambling in order to give strength to your argument.

You'd need to be careful not to:

- focus only on the inaccuracies or accuracies of the view;
- assess the view, but not give clear examples to back up your assessment;
- spend so long debating the view that you forget to draw a clear conclusion about its validity.

The wrong rules

Just because I'd thrown out my fuddy-duddy scholar didn't mean I knew what I was doing with essay writing. Not being scared of something and actually being good at something are completely different things. Without the little old man inside my head, my writing got better but it took a long time for it to get good. For a while, I continued to write according to some misguided rules I'd created about essay writing.

X Your essay should include everything you know about the topic. WRONG!

This was my downfall for a number of essays. I thought that if I incorporated every idea mentioned in lectures into my essays, my lecturers would see how diligent I'd been about coming to class and would reward me for it. In my efforts to come across as well-read and versatile, I'd weave completely irrelevant ideas into my essay. Rather than adding to my essay, these ideas just detracted from my main point, resulting in a vague mish-mash of disconnected themes.

X Your own opinion should be the core of your essay. NO WAY!

In hindsight, this one's a no-brainer. There I was, a newbie to the academic world and I thought that *my* opinion was important enough to warrant a full essay? When I got better at essay writing I realised it was my readings that needed to be the core of my essays; I could have an opinion, sure, but only in response to the readings. I was in no way qualified to make sweeping statements about the state of the world; at undergraduate level it is quite enough to suggest tentatively the strengths and limitations of what more educated people think about an issue.

X **Your essay needs to sound like the ones in the course reader. NOPE!**

Once again, an obviously false assumption on my part. The articles in the course reader were invariably written by super-intellectuals whereas I was a first-year student just getting my head around how to read academic writing properly. It made no sense for me to try to mimic it, so it's not surprising that I failed at it.

The right rules

By my second year, I'd got my head around the real rules I needed to follow in order to write a good essay.

✓ **Be humble**

As soon as I acknowledged who I really was as an author (new to the academic world and therefore relatively ignorant about academic matters), I started writing appropriately for my status. I learnt that the only way to sound intelligent as an undergrad is to find and write along the very fine line between sounding ignorant and informed. How to find this? Cover both sides of the argument, even if you favour one. Rather than stating your opinion, state the opinion of someone more cited than you and reference it. Be tentative: does your example really *show* or does it *suggest*? Can you say for sure that this *is* the case, or is it just the way it *seems* to you? Are you really in a position to make sweeping statements about what people are like, or how society functions?

As a general rule of thumb, reference anything that anyone could argue against.

✓ Write formally

As someone who shirked essays in favour of creative writing and journalism in Year 13, it took me a while to get the hang of the kind of formal writing expected in a uni essay. As I found in my first attempt, adjectives and fancy synonyms turn your essay into a minefield. Don't shorten anything – so no contractions (like it's, there's), spell out numbers under three digits long and avoid abbreviations (such as e.g., i.e.). Reword rhetorical questions as tentative statements so that 'So, what was Bronte's purpose in *Jane Eyre*?' becomes 'Bronte's purpose in *Jane Eyre* seems uncertain.'

✓ Don't discuss your essay in your essay

In the first week of uni, one of my lecturers was generous enough to tell the class that he would fail anyone who wrote 'this essay will'. Not all lecturers tell their students this, instead giving them average grades with vague mention of 'stylistic issues'. Don't begin your conclusion with 'in conclusion' and don't go on to tell your reader what 'this essay has' done. Don't remind your reader what was 'shown in the previous paragraph'. Your essay is not a piece of writing about your argument, it is your argument; establishing your voice outside the essay will only push your reader away. The important point here is also that it is better to be tentative rather than to suggest that because your essay says something it is therefore true, proven and wrapped up.

The process of writing an essay

The essay-writing process isn't just about writing an essay. It's about managing information; your job is to find, read, select, reference, interpret, interact with and then finally structure this information into a formal essay.

The process is restricted mostly at the beginning and the end; at the beginning, you are restricted by the essay question and your prior knowledge and at the end by the constraints of the formal essay structure. In the middle, you are restricted only by your creativity. However, the entire process of writing the essay should be subject to your own critical restrictions of making sure you are answering the question, and that you are doing so in a formal essay-writing style and within the required word limit.

Research

This is the 'expanding' part of the essay-writing process. Research is, as I've explained, the core of your essay as an undergrad; it should underpin everything you write, every conclusion you come to, every challenge you pose. For me, this was always the most exciting, daunting stage of the process. After choosing a question that appealed to me, it was exciting to read the books and articles that other people had written about the subject matter and issues involved. At the same time, though, it was daunting to realise that it would be impossible to read them all before the essay was due, let alone before my degree was completed.

Your main goal during this process is gathering information. You want to expand your research pool until you know how you are going to answer the question and can see how you're going to break down that answer into key points.

THE ESSAY-WRITING PROCESS

You begin with the constraints of the imposed material: lectures, set readings and question structure.

The expanding stage: you collect information, make notes, keep references, develop ideas and explore perspectives.

The stage of open, creative breadth: you group information, fill in the blanks, add your own thoughts and refer back to the question.

The contracting stage: you select the most useful information, refine your ideas, structure those ideas formally and edit.

You end with the constraints of the essay requirements: word limit, reference style and format strictures.

Start

First I'd open a new document and label it with the course code and essay topic, for example: *COMS102 – News Ownership essay.* I'd type my essay question and leave it at the top of the document so I wouldn't forget the question I was answering: *'Discuss how news proprietors can influence news content'*. Whatever you write, it *must* answer the question, otherwise you won't pass the assessment; having the question at the top of my page at all times stopped me straying from the task at hand.

Then I'd open a separate document and label it *Reference list.* Both this and the essay page were going to be evolving documents, added to every time I noted down something I wanted to include in my essay.

Read to understand

I'd get out my folder of article summaries and look through for anything relevant: in this case, anything involving news ownership, proprietor influence or bias in the news. Once I'd pulled out any relevant summaries, I'd jump online to a journal database and search for more articles. I'd then read and summarise those. Then I'd head to the library to do a catalogue search for the most relevant three or four books, reading and summarising the most relevant chapters from them. Before I even began writing, I'd want a pile of at least ten article or chapter summaries beside my computer and a good idea of how each one related to the essay question.

Read for information

Once I understood my sources, I'd search through them specifically for useful bits to use in my essay. Every time I came across an idea or quotation that I felt might be useful, I'd type it onto my document along with an in-text reference. In one chapter, for example, I came across the idea of media producers approaching the news with a business mentality. I found a quote that summed up this idea and typed it straight into my document: 'The industrialization of the news business in the nineteenth century resulted in the transformation of news into a mass-produced commodity' (Bettig and Hall, 2003, p. 75).

As I went, I'd type the full reference details of everything I was using into the *Reference list* document. The above short reference, for example, was followed up on my works cited page with one that looked like this:

> Bettig, R. and Hall, J. (2003). All the News that Fits: The News and Advertising Industries. *Big Media, Big Money* (pp. 73–108). Oxford: Rowman and Littlefield Publishers Inc.

Question the information

I'd keep doing this until I had a page or two worth of quotations. Then I'd stop and ask myself, 'What are these ideas telling me?' If I still wasn't sure, I'd read some more and pull out more ideas.

Writing

This is the 'open' stage of the essay-writing process, your peak period of creativity. Where before you've been gathering information, now you're going to start interpreting it, interacting with it and recontextualising it into the body of your essay. Where up until now the main input into the process has been from other authors, now your thoughts are the main input. This is the stage in which *you* have the most creative licence with your essay.

Group

If you've done enough research and questioned your findings, several common threads of thinking should have become apparent to you by now. I'd read through my page of notes again, cutting and pasting entries so that common ideas were grouped together. At this stage Bettig and Hall's idea would get grouped together with any other ideas I'd pulled out about proprietors influencing the news by using a business mentality. These groups would later become my paragraphs, so for a 1500- to 2000-word essay, I'd want five groups.

I'd give each 'idea group' a heading to represent the common theme amongst its points. I'd make sure that each heading answered the question in a different way; the group of ideas with Bettig and Hall's in it, for example, got the heading: *Proprietors' business approach influences the news*. (These headings would be deleted later.)

If my information wasn't evenly distributed across the different groups, I'd go back and gather a bit more information. By this stage in the game, researching would be much more structured; I'd know the idea that I wanted to expand upon further, and could do some specific online searches for the right kind of information. Once I knew that one of my paragraphs was going to be about proprietors abiding by principles of business rather than ethical broadcasting, for example, I was able to do a few online searches for 'news as a business' or 'business versus ethics in the newsroom' or 'media owner business agenda'. The extra information I found would flesh out my ideas until I had enough there for a paragraph.

I'd gather information until I had five evenly sized groups, each with about five referenced pieces of information or ideas in it, and a reference list that was at least ten sources strong.

Form sentences around the ideas

By this stage, I'd have a comprehensive 'plan' for my essay. A lot of essay writing guides will tell you to plan your essay at the beginning of the process; this is a good idea in an exam essay, when you've only got the information that is in your head, but in a research essay it's a waste of time. Research essays are about the research – how can you know what you are going to write about until you've done the research?

My plan at this stage would consist of my main ideas laid out in the form of headings and my academic evidence laid out in bullet-point form underneath these headings. All I would have done with the evidence at this stage was lift it out of its original source and into my document; what I needed to do now was to construct full sentences around the information I had and then join these sentences together.

At this stage, I wouldn't try to make things sound pretty. All I'd do is go through each group on my planning page and build sentences around the quotations. With weaving, the quotation I'd pulled straight out of the article –

> 'The industrialization of the news business in the nineteenth century resulted in the transformation of news into a mass-produced commodity' (Bettig and Hall, 2003, p. 75) –

became:

> According to Bettig and Hall, industrialisation has transformed news into a 'mass-produced commodity' (2003, p. 75).

Then I'd join up all the sentences in each group so that, rather than a list of bits and pieces, each heading would have under it a block of writing.

Make it yours

In front of me now would be the bare bones of an essay. All the key information would be there but it would be badly written with little flow. It would also be entirely other people's ideas and work. Now would be the time for me to inject a bit of myself. The key things to remember when putting other people's ideas into your own words are:

1. accuracy of translation – conveying the author's original message in your own words;
2. clarity of translation – using the minimum number of words in the clearest way to sum up their point;
3. honesty of translation – using language that's appropriate to you as a writer.

Then I'd question the information I'd referenced. Did I agree with it? Did I think its authors may have missed an important point? Could I compare or contrast two authors' points of view? Could I compare or contrast an author's point of view and my own? This is the part where I would interact with my evidence, by evaluating and comparing/contrasting the ideas I was referencing – a crucial stage in the BA essay-writing process. As I did so, I'd turn sentences like this –

> According to Bettig and Hall, industrialisation has transformed news into a 'mass-produced commodity' (2003, p. 75) –

into a series of sentences like this:

> According to Bettig and Hall, industrialisation has transformed news into a 'mass-produced commodity' (2003, p. 75). This description evokes an image of the news not as an objective source of information but as a commercial product designed first and foremost to attract a buying audience. Rohm shares this view and explains how contemporary proprietors must employ professional managers and globalise their investments to secure company profit and survival in the capitalist media market (2002, p. xi). Likewise, Gerald argues that encouragement from proprietors to select and present news for maximum financial gain reflects their desire for 'economic security' in the financially competitive modern world (1963, p. 19).

See what I did there? I developed that first point about news as a commodity, brought in a bit more information and then interacted with it. I showed my marker that I can see the implications of what Bettig and Hall are saying rather than just pasting their words into my essay. I showed the marker that I could compare Bettig and Hall's idea with those of other academics in order to make a stronger point.

Structuring and shaping

This is the 'contracting' stage of the journey. In front of you now is the product of your creativity, the fully grown extent of your research and ideas. You've done all the main thinking that you need to do, so now you can start to structure that thinking without sacrificing any of your creativity.

At this stage in the process, I'd usually have far too many words. Your lecturer will have set a word limit for your essay; this is a rule, not a suggestion. Generally speaking, most lecturers will overlook word counts which are within 10 per cent of the limit. Any more than that, though, and you're likely to lose marks. If you follow this model of essay writing, the challenge is not *to get enough* information and ideas, but *to cut them down* in order to present the most concise, clear and striking argument. The best way to start is by shaping your essay to fit the model of a formal university essay.

Tame it

An essay is a horse; let it run free and it's a dangerous thing, but break it in, force it to run around the paddock to the crack of your whip, and it'll serve you for life. What you've got in front of you now is a wild horse of an essay: it represents the energy, extent and strength of your research and ideas, without the structure it needs to meet formal essay requirements.

A lot of essay-writing guides will tell you to structure your essay from the beginning. To me, doing this limits creativity, flow and thoughts about thoughts. When teachers teach only to the assessment and concentrate on what 'has to be done', they snuff out potential for what 'could happen' along the learning journey. An essay is not just an assessment, it is an exploration into ideas and viewpoints and values. It's vital that you let yourself get immersed in the experience of it before you start shaping it to fit with assessment policy.

While it's important to give your ideas free reign at the start, it's crucial that you do structure them later on. An essay's structure is what sets it apart from any other piece of writing – if you don't get the structure right, you won't have written an essay. If you haven't written an essay, you won't pass. You need to tame your words, to edit them, and to see how sentences relate to other sentences and how paragraphs lead into other paragraphs. You need to train what you write to fit into this basic three-part structure: introduction, body paragraphs and conclusion.

Part One: Introduction

- Thesis statement (your answer to the question in one sentence)
- Description of thesis statement, definition of key terms
- Overview of the main points you are going to make

Part Two: Body paragraphs (three to seven, depending on the length of your essay)

Each one should have the following:

- Point (topic sentence – how this paragraph will answer the question in its own unique way)
- Explanation (one sentence to explain and clarify point)
- Examples and evidence (three-ish sentences)
- Analysis of examples and evidence (three-ish sentences, woven in with the evidence)
- Relevance of paragraph topic to essay question (one sentence)

This last point is extremely important.

Part Three: Conclusion

- Thesis statement reworded
- Overview of main points
- A sentence or two to leave your reader with something to think about

Work on your paragraphs first

Your introduction is there to overview the key points in your essay. You cannot know what these will be until you have written the essay. Consequently, you should write your introduction last. Since you've already got your paragraphs basically sorted out, focus on structuring them first.

Point

The first thing I'd do would be to turn my headings into topic sentences. A paragraph's topic sentence needs to convey the main point of that paragraph and link it to the essay question. At this stage in my COMS102 essay, I turned my initial heading – 'Proprietors' business approach influences the news' – into a more targeted, specific topic sentence that clearly answered the essay question and indicated what the paragraph was going to cover:

> Proficient business strategies see proprietors tailor news to make money.

Explanation

Next, I'd add in a sentence to explain the topic sentence further:

> Proficient business strategies see proprietors tailor news to make money. In a market driven by money rather than truth, such strategies have become essential to media survival in the modern economic world.

Examples

Here's where I'd include all the referenced material, reworked and reworded to show my understanding of it.

Analysis
If you've made the information yours already, your analysis will be wrapped up in the examples already.

Relevance
I'd reiterate how my examples answered the essay question:

> The resounding message from all of these descriptions is that news is a product, constructed by its owners for maximum profit.

Make it flow
The sentences in your paragraphs should now follow the essay paragraph structure: point, explanation, examples/analysis of examples, relevance. While your essay has to be structured, it also has to read well. Here's where you need to remember the real human being who'll be reading your essay – you want to make it as easy and enjoyable for them to read as possible.

First look at the flow between the sentences within your paragraphs. Read them aloud and notice the bits that jar. If two short, complete sentences are linked, try replacing the full stop with a semicolon. This works if the second part extends or explains the first; you can use a colon where the second more emphatically qualifies or gives an illustration of the first. Cut out unnecessary words and reword confusing sentences in the simplest possible terms. As a BA student, it's easy to produce complicated-sounding sentences, because this is what we're surrounded by all the time. You'll be rewarded for showing your ability to turn complex ideas into clear, easy-to-read sentences.

As you work on the flow of each paragraph, make sure that you have a variety of sentence lengths. A whole essay of long, over-punctuated sentences tends to drag on for your reader. A whole essay of short, minor sentences is just as hard to read. Aim for a good mixture and keep reading it aloud to yourself to check that it flows well. Take out the quotations or ideas that don't fit – at this point it's about valuing quality over quantity and cutting out the surplus stuff from your research. Remember that it's not your job to tell your marker everything you know about this topic.

When each paragraph flows nicely, step back and look for a logical flow *between* the paragraphs. Just like the sentences within your paragraphs, the paragraphs themselves need to flow naturally on from each other: the goal is to have your reader be able to read through the whole essay without having to stop to make sense of anything.

At this stage, I'd rearrange my paragraphs so that the basic ideas came at the start of my essay, building up to more complex ideas later on. You want to warm your reader up slowly, to build them up over the course of your essay so that when they hit the good stuff, they're well prepared for it.

Then I'd add in little links between the paragraphs so the transition between them was smooth and natural. In order for me to move between my paragraph about news as a business and my next paragraph about resource allocation, for example, I arranged the joining sentences like this:

> [end of news-as-a-business para] The resounding message from all of these descriptions is that news is a product, constructed by its owners for maximum profit.
>
> This product is then shared between news owners, allowing them to share the costs of production but ultimately sacrificing news diversity . . . . [start of resource allocation para]

By ensuring that the first sentence of the resource allocation paragraph alluded back to the news-as-a-business paragraph, I'd created a flow between them. As you craft these links between your paragraphs, keep reading them aloud to yourself to make sure that they sound right.

Now for the introduction

You know what your essay is about. *Now* you can write your introduction. The opening sentence needs to capture your audience, answer the question and lead into your argument. Easy. I started my COMS201 essay like this:

> In a digitised world, media proprietors influence news content by selecting news according to profit value rather than social significance.

This opening sentence gets to the point. It outlines the argument without giving too much away. It begs some explanation. It answers the question (how do news proprietors influence news content?) and so is a thesis statement. I always liked to have my thesis statement right at the beginning of my introduction. Some people put it at the end of the intro but I like the honesty of putting my cards on the table right from the beginning.

After the opening sentence, I explained it, defined any key terms and indicated the focus of my essay – which in this case used Rupert Murdoch as a case study of a media proprietor.

> In a digitised world, media proprietors influence news content by selecting news according to profit value rather

> than social significance. The paradox of media capitalism is that consumers both control and are controlled by proprietor profit. Ratings reflect the ability of manipulated news to fulfil the desires of the public, who adhere to the financial agendas of shareholders at the cost of truthful news. As 'the most entrepreneurial of all media titans' (Rohn 2002, p. xi), Rupert Murdoch's global expansion demonstrates some of the ways in which proprietors can influence news content and the implications of this intervention for the unregulated and largely foreign-owned New Zealand media market.

I then outlined what my essay was going to cover:

> While the ways in which proprietors can influence news content are plethoric, Murdoch's management is one of the world's clearest examples of how direct newsroom intervention, proficient business strategies, cross-media resource allocation and advertising are used by media owners to exert their power over news presentation.

I then added a final sentence to demonstrate the relevance of my essay to the wider society:

> Murdoch's ownership demonstrates how these strategies affect not only media integrity but also the democratic ideals of New Zealand society.

Three rules for introduction writing

- Make it interesting. Although your intro isn't the first paragraph you write, it's the first paragraph your reader reads. It needs to capture their attention and propel them forward into your essay.
- Clearly outline your points. If it's not clear, you're likely to throw your reader off before they've even had a chance to get started.
- Limit references. Only reference if you are defining key points, not to back up your argument.

Finally, your conclusion

Conclusions conclude. They wrap up everything you've said. Where your introduction needs to convince your reader to read your essay, your conclusion needs to convince them that it wasn't a waste of their time. I'd start by recapping my main points:

> Proprietor influence over news content through direct and opinionated intervention, businesses strategies, resource management and utilisation of advertising not only allows the expansion of media corporate powers but also restricts the entry of new players into modern media markets.

I'd then remind my reader what I'd showed them through these points:

> This stifles media diversification and violates public expectations of representative, objective and truthful news. Industrialisation and globalisation have shifted the role of New Zealand media from a public service designed to inform and support democratic society, to a corporate monopoly

> seizing opportunities for financial gain over chances to investigate, report and inform. The repercussions of this shift have serious implications for a society powerless against the manipulation of news by profit-driven proprietors. Cross-media ownership means proprietors hold influence over a wide selection of news and, as the numbers of media owners dwindle, media power is distributed amongst billionaire minorities.

I'd then throw in a final sentence to leave the reader with something to think about:

> In the hands of these few minorities, fair representation and media integrity fall victim to financial gain whilst the goals, agendas and intentions of the whole media world are reconfigured.

Three rules for conclusion writing

- Don't include any new information, just new perspectives on the information you've used in your essay.
- Don't just copy your introduction – reword your overview so that it sounds fresh.
- Conclude. Draw a conclusion that you haven't yet fully made in your essay. Keep this specific to what you've discussed – no sweeping statements or generalisations.

Titles: The icing on the cake

I wish I'd known this one earlier. Sadly, I only really got the hang of titles during my second year at uni, meaning that the COMS102 essay I use as an example in this chapter is conspicuously lacking one. In hindsight, I would have named it something like this:

> Money for nothing: how modern news is shaped by greed rather than truth

It's short, snappy and, most importantly – it has a subtitle. All good titles have a subtitle. Puns, alliteration and irony are optional but effective extras. As a creative writer, my titles became the place where I could have a little fun: although I tried to convey a clear sense of where the essay was going in the second half of the title, the few words before the colon were mine with which to entertain, intrigue and impress.

Your essay's title is the icing on the cake – not at all necessary but a delicious, pretty element to set your essay aside from the rest.

The final stages

Edit

I'll never forget the first time I saw a mistake on my CV. I was sixteen and had just spent two weeks delivering my CV to every reception desk in town. I'd tried different outfits, different hairstyles, different voices. I'd changed the font of my CV five times. I'd tried accountancy firms and warehouses but still I hadn't had a phone call.

In desperation, I took my CV to Mum and asked her what I was doing wrong. Was it the fact that I only had my restricted driver's licence? Was my experience as a sandwich maker detrimental to my search? Should I have stuck with Times New Roman after all? She took one look at the second page and laughed. She asked me if I could see what was so funny. I looked. Was it my discreet border? Were the bullet points too large? I didn't see.

'It's right here,' she said, pointing to the giant heading at the top of the page. Proffesional Record. Yeah. What's so funny about that? She looked at me, eyebrows raised, and told me to look again. I saw. I held my hands up to my face. The irony. The cruel, cruel irony of misspelling 'professional' in an application for typist jobs. It's not that I didn't know how to spell professional, I just hadn't been able to see my own mistake.

Editing – close, microscopic editing – is crucial. Editing means seeing each word for what it is, making sure it's the right one (spell checks don't pick up correctly spelt but out-of-context words – they don't think) and making sure it's in the right place. Editing sorts out the As from the Bs and can raise a barely-passing C to a comfortable B. Editing is your chance to show your marker/ employer that you are not a dumb-ass. Editing gets you the job.

Following the feedback on my first essay, my primary focus when editing was always clarity. I was lucky enough to receive this advice early on from one of my lecturers, advice that echoes through my mind every time I'm editing: 'Your ideas may well be gold but if I can't be bothered to decode them, they'll be marked as mud.'

Your marker doesn't have the time or the patience to spend their whole evening working out what you are trying to say. Your essay is only worth what they can easily get out of it, so you need to make it as easy as possible for them to get to the good bits. You need to serve the good bits up on your marker's plate, then take a knife and fork and feed each sentence to him or her, piece by piece.

How to do this? Just as you did when you were working on the flow of your paragraphs, you need to read each of your sentences aloud again and identify the parts that aren't 100 per cent clear. This time, though, you need to look at them under a microscope. If a sentence seems even slightly hazy this close up, it will be unreadable to your marker.

When you edit, you need to ensure that your essay:

- has a good mix of short and long sentences;
- has a good mix of active and passive sentences (passive: 'one argument for this is . . .' , active: 'Smith argues . . .');
- has a variety of sentence forms;
- makes its points with the minimum amount of words – if you find that you're trying to 'flesh out' your word count by using four words where one would do, you need more content – go back and do some more reading;
- uses simple words – remember, *you* are the author, not some old fuddy-duddy;
- uses formal language – you need to use words that you're familiar with, but steer clear of any slang, colloquialisms (casual, conversational language), contractions or abbreviations;
- uses the best word for the purpose – be specific, and use a thesaurus to help you pick the best word, but don't choose anything that you don't fully understand;
- uses accurate nouns and descriptive verbs rather than adjectives.

Proofread

Read it through again, this time checking every word. Always proofread on hardcopy – somehow having your words on the screen allows errors to become invisible. Things to watch out for when proofreading:

- Spelling. Use spell check. Make sure that you use English rather than American spelling, even if your computer may not recognise it (that's recognise, not recognize).
- Don't rely on the spell check.
- Typos. Use your proofreading microscope to scan for right words in the wrong context – e.g. 'their' where it should be 'there'.
- Punctuation. Make sure that you've used full stops, semi-colons, colons, dashes or commas properly. Watch out for 'comma splicing' – commas chucked into the middle of a sentence without any purpose. Check your use of apostrophes.
- Paragraph breaks. Check that your ideas are organised into paragraphs, with clear breaks between them.

Abide by the red tape

After checking to make sure that my essay complied with the rules of the English language, I'd check to make sure it fitted with the guidelines of my subject.

Each subject has its own essay-writing guidelines that you need to find, read and abide by. To follow the red tape of your subject guidelines, you may have to adjust a number of elements of your essay, such as:

- what font and size text you use;
- how you indicate paragraph breaks;
- how wide your margins are;
- how much spacing you have between the lines of text;

- how your title page should be laid out;
- how your header and footer should be laid out;
- where the page numbers sit;
- what referencing style you use;
- how you present longer quotations in your essay.

Make it pretty

How much freedom you have over how your essay looks will depend on how strict your course's essay-writing guidelines are. Provided you've met all these, you can make it pretty. Not too pretty, mind – a formal essay is not the place for decorative borders and clip art. It's about complementing your essay with a professional, tidy presentation and showing your marker that you care about the details.

Font is a big deal. I really believe that the font someone writes in has an effect on the way the marker reads it. Font creates a first impression – and we all know how hard those can be to get rid of. It goes without saying that for a formal essay you want to use a formal font. Use your discretion here – Times may seem characterless but Comic Sans MS screams primary school. Arial might be flat and uncharismatic, but Curlz MT is way too . . . well, curly. If you have the choice, go for something you consider timeless, classic and appropriate to the assignment. If you can't decide, you can't go wrong with Times New Roman.

If there are no layout rules for your course, it's a good idea to leave about a three to three and a half centimetre-wide margin on both sides of your essay – this gives your marker space to write notes. My aim was always to make it as easy as possible for my marker to comment; feedback is crucial for learning and the reality is that markers often have enormous workloads and many will gladly take any opportunity to get through your essay a little quicker.

Unless you've been instructed otherwise, double-space your lines. This makes the text a lot easier to read and, again, gives extra space for comments. I always put a header and footer on my essays – the header would contain my student number and the course code and the footer would contain the page numbers, aligned to the right for easy viewing. This looked good and protected me when a page of my essay fell out and got mixed into the other 400 pages in the essay return box.

Whether the essay-writing guidelines required one or not, I'd make a title page. If my course provided a cover sheet, I'd put that on top but I'd always have my own title page immediately on top of my essay. On it I'd include (in this order) the course code, my lecturer and/or tutor's name, the due date, my name, my student number, the word count of my essay (if required) and, of course, its title.

Check your referencing

A lot has gone on since the researching stage of your essay, so it pays to double-check that all of your referencing is in order. Make sure that you've consistently followed the rules of your subject's referencing style right the way through your essay. Also make sure:

1. you've provided references for all fact-based information or ideas that aren't basic common sense;
2. you've fixed up generalisations such as 'everyone watches television' by referencing some research showing that the majority of New Zealanders watch television;

3. you've correctly referenced anything, quoted or paraphrased, that you've taken from other people's work, both in text and at the end in a list of references.

If at this stage you find that one of your references is missing a page number, check the internet before removing the quote entirely. Most journals can now be found online; and the good people at Google have digitised millions of books too. Although you may not be able to see the whole book, you can search for your quote and see what page number it is on. Just make sure that you reference the correct edition of the book, as that will probably affect the page number.

It's crucial that you get the referencing right because failure to do so can result in your being charged with the worst offence in the academic world: plagiarism. Plagiarism is, in essence, cheating: taking someone else's words or ideas and making them out to be your own. Although technically it's academic theft, plagiarism is murder to academics, and those in positions of power will take great pleasure in dealing you the harshest possible penalties for it – failing your assignment or sometimes even kicking you out of university altogether.

Avoid plagiarism

I'm not suggesting that you're the type of person to cheat, but I am suggesting that human beings are very capable of overlooking mistakes. You can sign all the honesty declarations you like (and most courses will expect you to, and to hand one in with your essay), but if you really aren't aware that you've plagiarised then such procedures are not going to help. This is why it's so crucial to take clear references right from the initial reading stage: it's very easy for ideas to be paraphrased so many times that they really start looking and sounding like your own.

A lot of courses now expect electronic submissions of essays. This allows your marker to run the essay through a plagiarism-checking programme such as Turnitin, which will scan your essay and look for similarities between it and a huge database of online texts. That means everything from online journal databases to Wikipedia to Google books and even previously submitted assignments. After your first essay submission, you'll be issued with a plagiarism report that will highlight the matches it found and give you a plagiarism percentage.

My first report told me that 30 per cent of my essay was plagiarised. My essay was streaked with so many different colours it looked like a Jackson Pollock painting. After closer inspection, though, under every stroke of Turnitin's brush was a quotation that I had referenced perfectly. The system finds matches; it's not smart enough to tell if the matched material has been correctly referenced or not. All my 30 per cent reflected was the fact that I'd used a lot of direct quotations – an issue that probably needed highlighting, but was hardly criminal.

Leave it

Put it away. Seriously. If you've made enough time for your essay, you'll have a few days up your sleeve now to let it settle. Save your essay in three places and go work on something else for a while.

Proofread and, if necessary, edit again

I hoped that having a few days apart from my essay would give me a different perspective on it. When I came back to the essay, I'd read the hardcopy as if I was a marker. It always seemed like a new essay – the combination of time passing and reading it after reading other things really helped me to see it more objectively.

I'd go through with a red pen and mark the mistakes, inconsistencies and patches of ambiguity. Then I'd go back to the computer, fix up the issues and print it out again. Then I'd give my essay away.

Give it away

By this stage in the game, my essay and I would have a very close relationship. We'd have spent at least two or three weeks together, for hours on end every day. It would have witnessed my full range of emotions from joy to anger to outright frustration. It would have watched me eating breakfast every morning and it would have been the last thing I saw before I went to bed each night. By this stage, we'd be tight.

I don't want to be melodramatic, but when I gave my essay away at this stage I would feel a little tug on my heart. It hurt. Giving it away, however, was a crucial stage in the crafting process; it allowed an objective person to read it through and say what they thought. No matter how many days you have apart from your essay, you can never get this kind of objectivity. By this stage, you are hopelessly biased.

It's crucial that you choose someone who has written university-level essays themselves because only they understand the style and standard that are expected. Remember that they can comment on presentation and clarity, but they can't tell you what to write – getting someone else to write your essay for you is called 'ghost writing' and is a major offence at uni.

Taking feedback is one of those life skills that no one prepares you for, like looking after an intoxicated friend or dealing with a broken heart: all of a sudden you're thrown into a new and very uncomfortable situation and there's no one there to tell you how to handle yourself. The first time Blake gave me feedback I handled myself by throwing a tantrum.

His tactlessness is both a blessing and a curse. By telling me exactly what he thought of my essay, he gave me an honest, objective outsider's opinion. He gave me a clear, completely unsugarcoated description of how my essay came across to him – where it fell flat, where it lost meaning and where it made no sense whatsoever. The downside of this priceless insight was that at the beginning it was very, very painful.

I gave my first essay to Blake out of frustration: I'd received the same comments about lack of clarity three essays in a row. By 'gave', what I mean is that I printed it out, threw it in his direction, unleashed a stream of disclaimers and then dashed out of the house for an hour or so. To think of someone else reading and critiquing that essay made me feel the same way I did in that recurrent dream of being naked in a crowd of people with only a handkerchief to hide behind. Vulnerable beyond words.

After throwing him my essay, I'd gone out and walked around the CBD for over an hour. I did the loop around Oxford Terrace, Madras, Gloucester and Colombo four times and then once I'd been walking for an hour did one more as a precaution. When I got home, he was still scribbling furiously. As I hovered in the doorway to the bedroom, he looked up and smiled briefly.

'I'll let you know when I'm finished,' he said, then returned to the pile of papers in his lap.

I was making a cup of tea when he called me back. I left the bag brewing and tiptoed into the bedroom. Blake looked up and patted the patch of bedspread beside him. He told me to take a seat.

'I've got to be honest with you, Rebecca.'

I nodded.

'I don't like this essay.'

I felt my heart slide into my stomach. 'Why not?'

'It's not very good.'

I made a snatch at the essay but he raised it above my reach. 'What do you mean, it's not very good?'

'It's just not good, okay? You've got a lot of work to do on it.'

I grabbed my hair by the roots and clenched my eyes shut. 'But I've spent three weeks on it and it's due tomorrow! I can't spend any more time on it!'

'Well, just hand it in like it is, if you like. I just don't think you'll get a very good mark.'

A lone tear sprang out of my eye. 'Why do you have to be so mean?'

'I'm not being mean, I'm just telling you how it is. Look, I've spent over an hour on this thing, Rebecca. If you didn't want my feedback, you shouldn't have asked for it.'

He bundled up the pile of papers and held them out to me. On the front page, I could see a giant question mark, some heavy crosses, a couple of illegible comments. I felt an overwhelming urge to push the papers back at him and walk away. Before I could do so, Blake gently pushed the bundle into my hand and winked. Then he picked up his laptop and started playing solitaire.

I stared at the wad of paper for a minute or so and then stomped off to my study space, where I chucked it in the bin. Then I cried and threw some course readers about the room for a while. Blake, wisely, left me to it.

After a while, I pulled the essay out of the bin and read Blake's comments. He'd indicated a number of places where my writing was unclear. He'd circled some typos. There was one paragraph with a giant question mark right the way through it but, other than that, his comments were mostly positive. I read the essay again and totally agreed with what he'd said about it.

By the time Blake came to let me know that dinner was ready I'd reworded everything in clearer terms. I left the essay in the study and followed Blake into the lounge, where he'd set up a bowl of nachos and two beers on top of the old heater we used as a table. He'd made the nachos with potato wedges rather than corn chips, just the way I like them. He'd got the dodgy aerial set up so that we could watch *Lost* with the minimum amount of static.

Once *Lost* was over, I went and got the new essay.

'Much better,' he said, picking at a potato wedge left in the bowl.

'So you like it now?'

He handed it back, smiled and took a swig of his beer. 'No, not really. But it's much better than it was.'

Although Blake didn't like the essay, my marker did and gave me an A+ for it. He commended my clarity and my 'thoughtful, well developed' ideas. While liking an essay is subjective, understanding one is not. The parts I'd changed after seeing Blake's giant question marks were the ones my marker praised for being clear and precise. From then on, I ignored Blake's subjective comments about my essays and focused only on his objective pointers.

Know when to trust your own judgement

I once heard about a guy who makes guitars for a living. Apparently, a guitar needs so many layers of polish that he never knew that it had enough until he'd applied one layer too many. This story made me think of the sunsets I used to watch in Southeast Asia – I'd never know that the colours were at their brightest, the light reaching the farthest, the whole show at its absolute most jaw-dropping, until they started to fade.

Essays are the same. Following Blake's advice on clarity, my essays improved steadily throughout my first year. He started saying that he didn't have much feedback to give me, that my essays were fine the way they were. 'Just give me whatever you can,' I'd say, 'they can always be better.'

Blake did as I asked, and suggested areas where I could develop my ideas further, or reword them in more mature language. I did as he suggested.

I stopped pushing Blake for pointers when I found that by following them, I'd cost myself a mark. My marker explained that I'd pitched a first-year essay too high, that I'd tried to include far too much information in my 1500 words. The essay would have been clearer, she explained, had I just stuck to the key concepts of the course.

An essay can only be so clear before it starts getting muddled again. Blake's input had helped me to identify the parts of my writing that I needed to develop and, as a result, had been instrumental in my reaching top essay marks. Once I had done that, though, I didn't need his feedback anymore. Now it was up to me to improve my essay-writing skills as I progressed through uni. I was independent.

Get rid of it

Your essay will never be finished. You will never get 100 per cent. Either you will reach the end of your ability, or you will run out of time. In either case, it is time to get rid of your essay.

All too often, I left it to the last minute to print out my final copy. It's as if I wanted to give my mind every spare minute I could to think of the clincher line that would get me an A+. What I came to learn is that nothing productive happens in the final half hour before the essay is due. I'd go onto the computer to print it out and I'd see a mistake. I'd get frantic, not read the paragraph properly and convince myself that it was unclear. I'd try to rewrite it and get myself confused about what the point of the paragraph was in the first place. I'd end up scrawling something down that was nowhere near as good as what I'd originally written, then have to join the printing queue with only three minutes to spare before the deadline.

Without fail, within those three minutes my printing account would run out, or the printer would run out of ink, or my computer would crash. Anything that could go wrong with the world would go wrong in those three minutes. The only place you want to be during those three minutes is in front of the essay dropbox, or in the pub celebrating. Even one minute past the deadline can result in you losing precious marks.

What I came to accept was that anything that I hadn't thought of in the hour before my essay was due just wasn't going to make it in. I'd ensure that my essay was finished the night before and then I'd trust my judgement. I would tell myself that any thoughts I'd have in the stressful minutes before delivery time could never be as logical as the thoughts I'd had last night in the calm environment of my study space. After all the effort I'd gone to with my essay, the thought of losing points for lateness was too painful to risk.

Once it was printed (preferably half an hour before the due time), I'd get it clamped by the freaky library staplers, then I'd escort it up to the essay dropbox. I'd give it a little kiss (crucial stage in the process) then push it in, peering in after it to check that it had made it onto the pile. I'd say goodbye. I'd walk away.

The aftermath

The essay crafting process doesn't end when you hand it in. The hand-in date represents the turning point in the process: while up until now it's been about creating the best essay you can, from this point onward it's about reflecting on what you did. Feedback is crucial to improvement. No matter how much you may want to move on from your essay, do justice to the hard work you put into it by going back and learning from it.

Get it back

Getting it back takes forever. I found it easiest to pretend that I was never going to see my essay again. In some courses, markers have over a hundred essays to mark; with each one taking at least half an hour to get through, that's a fair amount of evenings spent poring over essays. The rings of red wine or coffee that accompanied my returned essays were testament to these long hours.

Don't look at it until you're ready. I was never ready until I had found an empty room or quiet stairwell in which I could read it alone. Sometimes the essays would be given out in tutorials, in which case I'd file mine into my bag for later. Sometimes my lecturer would ask that they be collected from the office, in which case I'd take it from the receptionist and then go and find a quiet corner before looking at it. In hindsight, this sort of behavior was probably a good sign that I was taking my degree seriously – that I cared about my marks but was humble enough to know that good ones were by no means a certainty.

After learning how to take feedback from Blake, I usually found it pretty easy to accept my marker's notes. Feedback, whether you agree or disagree with it, is a gift. It is a priceless insight into how someone else views your work. It turns your essay into a real piece of literature with which someone else can interact. Never forget that your marker's comments aren't personal – whether you pass or fail is of little consequence to them. They are reading your essay for the first time and are commenting on it as an outsider trying to look into the world you have created.

Celebrate where your essay has succeeded – the parts that made the somebody who marked it nod enough to tick the margin, or smile enough to write 'Interesting point!' or 'Insightful'. As much as it might sting, acknowledge the parts where it didn't work so well. Find and pay attention to the sentences that made somebody confused enough to scribble a question mark in the margin, or to ask you a clarifying question at the bottom of the page. Think about how you'd rewrite those parts, and what you'll do differently in your next essay to ensure that the same issues don't crop up again.

As hard as it can be to accept feedback, any feedback is preferable to none at all. The one time this happened was the one time I took it back: I didn't mind getting a B+, I explained, but I just wanted to know how I got it – the grade was the only thing my marker had written on my essay. I left it with the course coordinator, who had it back to me the next day. This time, the paper was dotted with notes and the grade at the end had turned into an A. She apologised profusely and we shook hands, both knowing that the previous marker hadn't even read it. Only take your essay back if you're absolutely sure, though, as I have heard of people's marks going down as a result of remarking.

More important than its grade, however, is your essay's percentage mark. Academic transcripts don't list the grades you get for each individual essay and exam, but one grade for the course. Marks get added up and averaged out. So, say your first essay gets a B+ with a score of 79 per cent and your second essay in that course gets an A with a score of 81 per cent, there's only 2 per cent between them – and together they'd average out to 80 per cent each – which would make an average mark of A. If you're worried about grades, remember to keep your essay marks in the context of your overall average.

Once I'd read through my essay, I'd store it somewhere safe. I'd always read my marker's comments again before starting my next essay; good markers make their own notes and reward students who actively improve on the areas they highlighted last time. You may be a small fish in a big pond, but you're a fish whose work they've spent at least half an hour on and they will remember their own comments. How much you improve in your essay writing depends on how well you can take their feedback.

Step 8
Conquer exams

Conquer exams – sound like an oxymoron to you? Like something you could never, ever hope to achieve? You are wrong. You can dominate exams. Pretty much anyone can, provided that they find a strategy that works for them.

I found my strategy by the end of my first semester. I'd never done well in high school exams, writing screeds of irrelevant, unstructured drivel or, worse still, writing nothing at all. Once I wrote a whole novel essay in response to a question about a film. As soon as I'd finished the essay I noticed what I'd done and proceeded to scrunch my whole paper up in the middle of the exam, forcing everyone to break their train of thought and acknowledge my pain. I can be pretty immature like that sometimes.

I didn't beat myself up about it. Exams just weren't me.

I realised that exams were going to have to be me halfway through my first year at uni. I'd spent a whole semester overcoming academic challenges and by this time my essays were bringing in consistently high marks. The thought of these marks – the symbols of all I had fought to overcome – being wiped out by bad exam results made me feel sick.

I'd put off thinking about exams all semester, hoping that by pushing them out of my mind, I might be able to push them out of my life. Then, towards the end of Semester 1, I received an email letting me know that my examination dates had been set. I would be sitting exams in a few weeks' time and, as much as the thought made my belly flip, I had no other choice than to accept it. As I sat in front of my computer, a prayer Mum used to recite when I was freaking out about Athletics Day or a driving test popped into my head:

> God, grant me the serenity to accept the things I cannot change, courage to change the things I can, and wisdom to know the difference.

I'm not religious, but this prayer always made a lot of sense to me. I could not change the fact that I was going to have to sit exams. I was going to have to change the way I thought about them.

Pre-prep

When it comes to exams, you need to prepare to prepare; the preparation is so important that it needs preparation in itself. The main goal of this pre-preparation is getting over your hatred of exams and embracing your new strategy for conquering them.

Stop moaning

Let me guess – you're bad at exams too, right? You can handle essays, take-home tests and research assignments, but when it comes to exams, you just flunk. You read through all your notes beforehand but once you get in there, nothing comes out. The very thought of exams makes your stomach turn. You're *just not good at exams*. End of story.

How'd I know? Ninety per cent of students have the same story. Get a new one.

After committing to changing my outlook on exams, I decided that my story was going to be that I was scared of exams because I didn't know how to prepare for them but that once I worked out how to ace them, I'd be sweet. Sweet. That's what I'd be once I worked out my strategy. The strategy was the only thing standing between me and exam victory.

Sort your head out

By the time I got to my first set of exams, I was knackered. I'd had so many things to get used to, so many people to meet, so many skills to learn and practise that I was spent. I'd crafted two essays for each of my courses and each one had stripped me of a large chunk of my energy. My head was so full of theorists and ideas and quotations that I couldn't tell one from the other anymore. The thought of preparing for exams put me to sleep.

When I'm flustered, I tidy. If I can't tidy up the mess in my mind, I tidy up my house and hope that it'll set some kind of example for my brain to follow. As it was academic clarity I was after, I started on my study space. I cleared out my satchel and filed all my notes away in ringbinders, which I labelled and put on my bookshelf. I went through my computer, labelling all my files clearly and deleting any duplicates. I pulled my course readers out of the various corners they'd made it into around the house and stacked them neatly on the shelves. I stapled together all the photocopies I'd made from books and placed them alongside. I looked up the exact dates of all my exams and put them onto my diary, along with one- and two-week reminders.

Then I ditched uni work for a couple of days. Lectures were over for the term so I spent a few days catching up with my family and friends. I went shopping. I cleaned out the laundry. I went for long walks. I didn't feel at all guilty.

Sort your body out

Students are renowned for their poor diets. Being a student himself when we met, Blake had brought his 'two-dollar-a-meal' rule into the relationship and I abided by this rule pretty faithfully for most of the time I was at uni. I always ate healthy meals but they tended to be erratic – as someone who was always anaemic and prone to low blood sugar, I tended to rely on long blacks for the energy I should have been sourcing from my diet.

The first coffee-fuelled test I had at uni was a disaster. The test was at 3 p.m., by which time I'd had three slices of bread and an apple to eat during the day and nothing since 11 o'clock that morning. The night before, our flat had lost power so I'd had cereal for dinner. En route to the test I grabbed a quadruple-shot coffee, which I threw back in three or four gulps. That'd see me right.

It was a multiple-choice test and I was alert for the first ten minutes. Then my hand started to shake. Then I needed to use the bathroom. Then I got dizzy and started to struggle to read the questions. My ticks went all wobbly. Then I felt exhausted. I rushed through the test and left early to get some fresh air.

I passed the test, but when I looked back over my answers it was obvious that most of my errors were due to a lack of concentration. I *knew* the answers, I just hadn't read the question properly, or I'd ticked the wrong box by mistake. Sitting a test required a whole different level of concentration to sitting in a lecture theatre, a level of concentration for which I was totally unprepared.

When exams came round, I paid a lot of attention to what I ate. I included protein in every meal and made sure to eat plenty of complex carbs – wholegrain breads, pastas and cereals. When I was feeling rundown during the day, I'd snack on a muesli bar instead of buying a coffee. I bought multivitamins from the supermarket and took one every day. I drank a lot of water and green tea. Whether I was experiencing the placebo effect or not, my concentration got a million times better; I had a lot more energy and stopped crashing at about 3 p.m. every afternoon like I used to.

As soon as I started seeing food as an investment in my success, I started eating better. Before every exam, I'd make sure to have a good meal then I'd have a muffin before I went in. Sure, I probably put on a couple of kilos, but it seemed a small price to pay for a lifetime's worth of good grades.

Identify and acknowledge your mistakes

Once my head was clear, I felt able to tackle the challenge in front of me: working out how I was going to do well in exams. I started by looking at my previous strategy and how it had gone wrong in the past.

Exams had always been, in my mind, the great unknown. Their content was top-secret information that no student could ever hope to lay their eyes on before examination day. As a high school student, I'd felt at the complete mercy of every exam and the questions it decided to throw at me. As a result, I studied widely and vaguely, reading through my school books from start to finish several times over and trying to memorise their content.

If someone had asked me to tell them everything I knew about any given topic before going into the exam, I'd have impressed them. As soon as I tried to answer a specific question on the topic, though, I'd freeze. The questions seemed irrelevant and confusing. Then, trying to convert the knowledge in my head into an essay format just threw me off completely.

Looking back on my previous attempts, I realised that I had made three major mistakes in my exam preparation. The first was being blinded by my fear of the unknown: by convincing myself that I couldn't possibly know what was going to be asked of me, I hadn't bothered to try and work it out. The second was studying too widely and trying to take in too much information: by memorising everything I'd been taught over the year, I'd cluttered up my brain entirely and prevented myself from being able to access the information I needed. The third was failing to study in the style in which I'd be expected to think in the exam: simply reading over my books and taking notes had left me totally unprepared for how I was going to convey this information in an essay format.

I couldn't change my previous exam marks. But I did have the courage to change the way I studied for exams from now on. And hey, the fact that I could see this meant – provided that the prayer was right – that I had a bit of wisdom on my side as well.

Devise your new strategy

By this stage, it was clear to me what I had to do:

1. learn what was going to be in the exam;
2. study only what was going to be useful in the exam;
3. study by writing essays, as most of my Arts courses would expect answers in essay form.

Your strategy will depend on what you find when you look at your past exam mistakes. It will depend on the type of person you are and the way you learn best. It will depend on how committed you are to becoming the sort of person who's good at exams.

My strategy may or may not be useful to you. You may want to use bits from it or nothing at all. My hope is that by sharing it with you, you will start thinking about how *you're* going to conquer exams and that you will believe me when I say that it is possible.

Study

Learn what's going to be in the exam

Not as hard as you'd think. Once I started to look into it, it became clear that there were three main sources of clues as to what my exam may hold in store for me: previous exam papers, lectures and tutorials, and conversations.

Previous exam papers

We are fortunate enough to have begun uni in the digital age. Everything is online. For me, this included exam papers for my courses and others like it from the previous three years. If you're not as lucky as I was, your uni will have these on file in hardcopy somewhere – ask your lecturer or a librarian where you might access them.

As soon as I began to look through the old papers, I began to see strong, clear themes emerging. Sometimes course coordinators would use the same questions, year after year. Sometimes they'd use the same questions every second year. Sometimes they'd use the same questions but reword them. Sometimes they'd use a number of new questions each year, but there'd always be a few questions that were the same as or very similar to questions asked in previous years.

It makes sense. If the course is the same, why would lecturers look for different learning from their students? Exam questions, I realised, aren't top secret. They are worded to let you demonstrate that you have learnt the basic information they want you to take away from the course. There's no mystery about them.

Lectures and tutorials

Not every lecture is relevant to the exam. Likewise, not all your notes are relevant for your study. Once I was familiar with the key topics in my courses, I was able to look back over my notes to the lectures that addressed those topics and see which direction the lecturer was taking it that year. So, for example, I now knew that the last three years' exams for COMS102 included a question about sports news as a genre. I looked back to my notes about sports news and saw that this year the lecturer had placed a lot of emphasis on the idea of 'sport as a commodity'. It seemed pretty obvious that this would be the focus of this years' exam.

The last lecture of the term is often a 'sum-up' lecture. Here the most important topics from the course are overviewed and the exam is foreshadowed. There is a very good chance that the topics a lecturer chooses to overview are those that are going to be in the exam. Some will make it even more obvious to you: as Dr Matheson discussed the exam in his sum-up lecture of COMS101, for example, a giant Mickey Mouse face flashed up onto the screen, lingered for a couple of seconds, then disappeared. I still have my notes from that lecture:

Note to self: Disney DEFINITELY in the exam!

Tutorials are there to ensure that students are getting their heads around the most important parts of the course. Any topic studied closely in tutorials is most likely going to be in the exam. Any topic overviewed on the last tutorial of the term is almost certainly going to be in the exam. Any topic that your tutor strongly advises you to study will definitely be in the exam.

Conversations

Lecturers can't tell their students what's going to be in the exam. And they won't. What I learnt, however, is that lecturers can sometimes advise on the areas about which they think you could do with some better knowledge. They can let a student know whether they think a study plan is comprehensive enough. They can talk to students more comprehensively about previous exam papers and the kinds of answers they expect. They can't, however, unfairly advantage one student over any other: if they give one student some helpful tips, a summary of that conversation will usually then be sent around the rest of the class.

Study what is going to be useful in the exam

You don't have to know everything. Trying to do so will only prevent you from learning the things you really do need. Fill your head up with hay and it'll be very difficult to find the needle. Fill your head with an artillery of needles and all you need to do in the exam is choose the right one for the job.

Having said this, I'd still start my study by reading over all of my notes for the course. It gave me a satisfying sense of ownership to thumb through the sheets of notes I'd collected, like an artist stepping back to take in her mural. Reading over my notes would leave me with a clear impression of what the course had been about, what the key ideas were and how they were linked. Even though you don't need to know a lot about topics other than the ones you focus on in the exam, casual links to other ideas show your marker that you totally get it.

Then I'd narrow it down. Most Arts exams require you to write three essays. I'd pick the three topics that I'd now know were going to feature in the exam, then I'd choose a fourth one as a backup. Having four topics totally sorted in my head allowed me to write on three and to use the fourth to make comparisons, links and contrasts. For each topic I was going to study, I'd pull out all my notes and compact them down onto half a page. For me, notes I just copied never made it into my memory – they needed to be summarised and put into my own words before my mind would accept them long term.

Study in the format you'll be expected to answer in

Would you sit your practical driver's test without ever having practised driving a car? Preparing for an essay exam by only taking notes is like preparing for your restricted driver's licence by only reading the *Road Code*. Bad idea.

You need to learn the theory and then practise in the medium in which you are going to be assessed. If you're preparing for a multi-choice test, learn the material and then practise using tests from DVDs or the internet. If you're preparing for a short-answer test, learn the material and then practise summarising that material into paragraphs. If you're preparing for an essay-based exam, like those set in most Arts courses, study the material and then practise writing essays about it. Here's how.

Put the information you want to remember into essays

I'd start by writing myself a broad, generic essay question for each of my four topics, using previous exam papers as a guide. Next I'd make an essay plan for each question, incorporating all the key information I'd summarised on my half sheet; then I'd turn each plan into a short essay. I'd make sure to follow the same basic paragraph structure as I did for my research essays, but I'd make the essays a whole lot shorter – keeping my intro short and sweet and sticking to one sentence for each of the Point, Explanation, Example, Analysis and Relevance parts of the paragraph.

I timed myself writing and found that I could handwrite about 1000 words in an hour. I knew that I would have three hours to write three essays, so I made sure that each of my practice essays was no more than about 800 words long. This would allow me fifteen minutes or so at either end to plan and edit. Everyone's writing speed is different, so you need to check your own and plan accordingly. Just remember that quality is always preferable to quantity in an exam; there's simply no time for waffling.

I'd refer to readings in my practice essay but only those studied in the course. I wouldn't bother referencing them properly either; in exam conditions, you're not expected to be nearly as thorough as you are in research essays. You need to remember the theorist's name – and a year might be handy but isn't essential. Include short, memorable quotations or paraphrase the theorist's main idea.

Keep your practice essays broad. Even though you may be sure that your topics are going to be in the exam, the question is going to be much more specific than 'discuss your chosen topic'. The purpose of the practice essays is not for you to memorise pre-written essays but to familiarise yourself with using the information you know to answer a range of questions on the topic, in the style of a formal essay.

Write out your essays until you remember them

Up until now I'd be working on the computer. Once I'd typed up my four practice essays, though, I'd copy them out onto refill. Then I'd write them out again, timing to see how long it would take me to write that many words. I'd then copy the essays out again and again until the key ideas, information and theorists within them were firmly engrained in my mind. Rather than chucking the information into my brain at random, I was filing it away in an ordered format.

I'd keep writing out my essays until I could remember them by heart. To save my fingers from getting too blistered, I'd alternate between handwriting and typing. I'd practise until I could say them out loud on command.

Practise using the memorised information to answer any question

Remembering the info, though, wasn't enough. I needed to be so comfortable with it that I could apply it to any question I might be asked about my topics. I needed to have the theories and the theorists wrapped around my little finger.

Back to the previous exam questions. I picked every question related to my topic and wrote an essay in response to each one. All the same information I'd memorised, minus a few irrelevant facts and with a few more relevant examples.

If I'm under pressure, it's easier for me to completely reword and recontextualise a memorised essay than to think of a new one on the spot. It's like the difference between turning a ham and cheese sandwich into a chicken and lettuce one – the structure's already there, and all I have to do is swap the ham for the chicken and swap the cheese for the lettuce and it's like a whole new sandwich. Easy.

Sit your own exams

Here's where I got really nerdy. I'd write five questions for each topic, with the help of previous exam questions and suggested questions from my lecturer. I'd put each set of five questions into a hat and then pull one out until I had three questions on the desk in front of me. I'd then grab a glass of water, let Blake know I'd be in an exam for three hours and shut the door.

I'd then sit my own exam. I'd lay my watch out on the table and set aside an hour for each essay, including planning and editing time. If I needed to go to the bathroom, this would be deducted from my three hours. If someone came to the door, I'd leave them there.

My friends would laugh at me. Blake would get frustrated. Even my parents started to suggest that I might be taking it too far. I ignored them. These were all people who had told me that they too were 'just bad at exams'. I wasn't that person anymore. I was someone who was scared of exams but also someone who could conquer their fears. I told myself that this was a temporary lifestyle, that my neurotic personality was only short term.

Disclaimer

My approach was not always popular with uni staff who found out about it. They saw my preparation as sneaky, my tactics as somehow underhand. It's always important to keep such views in context.

In an age of free speech and self-directed research, exam questions are one of the few sources of power that university bigwigs possess over students. They say that studying for anticipated questions defies 'the point' of exams because, for these sorts of people, exams aren't a chance for you to show what you know but a chance for you to show how creative you can be under unfamiliar conditions.

My view is that such people have forgotten what it's like to be trapped in a room for three hours, to face an exam paper that will be full of surprises and tricks, and then be asked to concentrate. They have forgotten how hard it is to be creative whilst watching the clock. They have forgotten how difficult it is to access information under time pressure unless it is stored in just the right way. Or perhaps they remember, and accept it. Perhaps they are *just not good at exams* either.

In any case, your job is not to listen to everything these people say. Neither is it to take everything I say as law. What I have told you is what worked for *me* and my particular way of thinking, how *I* decided to address my shortcomings in high school exams. Your strategy will depend on what you've found hard about exams in the past and what you think you need to do to train your brain to work better in them.

Chill

After weeks of this routine, I felt truly prepared for my exams. I was nervous about entering the exam room but for the first time in my life I was confident that I had done everything I could to prepare myself for it.

I'd have fleeting horrors about a completely unexpected essay question, then remind myself that I knew enough information to be able to answer just about any question. I'd look back over the previous exam questions and be reassured by their predictability. I'd remind myself that in Arts there are no 'right' or 'wrong' answers, as long as they are worded well and backed up with evidence.

The day before my first exam, I was still feeling nervous.

I looked up the exam room on the UC website, got on my bike and cycled over to uni. I found the room in which I'd be sitting the exam in on the following day. It was empty, so I went inside. I sat in one of the desks, middle centre and scoped out the room: round clock on the wall to my right with a cracked white surround; long whiteboard at the front with three hours broken down into fifteen minute increments, each one crossed out – a memento left from that morning's exam; buzzing light in the back left corner; dirty words scratched into the bench desks. I left the room and found the bathroom – first left then on the right-hand side of the corridor. I exited the building through the large swing doors, knowing that the next time I did so I'd be leaving my first uni exam behind me.

I got home, cooked a healthy dinner of fish and vegetables (no wine, just lots of water) and watched *Amélie* with Blake – our first time spent together for several weeks. I packed my bag with a drink bottle, my wallet with my student ID inside, a spare watch, my practice essays (in case I needed a final reminder before I went in), and eight pens in blue and black. The last measure was the product of Blake's neuroses rather than mine – that evening he told me about the exam in which each of his five pens ran out one after the other. I set two alarms – cellphone and analog clock (having heard horror stories of cellphone batteries dying the night before an exam) and switched off the light at 10 p.m. – very early for me.

In bed, I spent about fifteen minutes running through how the following morning would pan out. Now that I'd visited the exam room I could picture exactly where I was going; I imagined cycling onto campus then making my way to the examination room. I retraced the steps I'd taken earlier that day in my head. I fell asleep more excited than nervous.

On the day

Your weeks of preparation, your countless hours of study, the anti-social lifestyle you've lived for the past few weeks, all boil down to this day. Exams are mentally, emotionally and physically taxing, so you need to structure the whole day carefully to ensure your optimum success in them. It's about keeping calm and retaining faith in the strategy you've spent weeks crafting. It's about having a clear plan for everything – how to get to the exam, what to do inside it, how to cope afterwards – and sticking to those plans despite your nerves.

Stay in control

I woke up before my alarms and ran through my practice essays one last time. I had a big bowl of muesli then grabbed my bike out of the airing cupboard and wheeled it outside. I knew that the chances of a bike puncture would be at their peak on the morning of my first exam so I wanted to get to campus at least half an hour before my exam started, whatever disasters happened. Bear in mind that Murphy's Law applies to car batteries going flat and buses running late, so always make sure to leave plenty of time to get to your exam; missing a bus or having your car break down are not accepted excuses for lateness.

Once on campus, I stopped in at the Law café to grab a cheese scone, which I ate as I looked over my practice essays one last time. Then I headed to the exam room. I arrived outside fifteen minutes early. I should have made it ten. My classmates were already milling about in droves, chattering about how nervous they were. I heard a guy talking about how he'd heard that news ownership – one of my four topics – wasn't going to be in the exam. My stomach turned. I ran off to the bathroom.

After splashing some water on my face I reminded myself that this guy couldn't possibly know what he was talking about. I reminded myself that even if he did, I had three other topics up my sleeve. I reminded myself that the information I had in my head could be applied to many topics other than the four I'd targeted. I would be fine. I didn't need to be infected by the general panic, the 'I'm no good at exams' attitude. It's never helpful and it's never supportive. I headed to the examination room.

Settle in

A tiny, pearl-encrusted old woman opened the door. I smiled at her and her eyes passed over me disdainfully. I'd heard about these 'invigilators' – rumour had it that the university kept them locked in a closet, releasing them only twice a year for exam supervision. An old man in a cardigan handed me a piece of card as I entered and told me to switch my cellphone off and leave it in my bag at the front of the classroom. I retrieved my pen stash, my ID and my water bottle from my satchel and followed the number on my card to the corresponding seat in the theatre – not far at all from where I'd sat the day before.

The exam paper had bet me there. It sat on the table in front of me, closed but tantalisingly transparent. I resisted the urge to hold it up to the light. A second old lady saw me looking at the cover and screeched a warning, to which I smiled politely in response. It stood to reason that the poor dear's nerves would be frayed. I pushed the exam paper away and started filling in the cover sheet.

Next, the old man in the cardigan withdrew a whiteboard marker from his chest pocket and wrote in giant letters on the whiteboard – CHEATING IS NOT ALLOWED. For the first time in my life, sitting in my first university exam, I realised what an interesting statement that is. I spent a good minute contemplating whether cheating would still be cheating if it *was* allowed, but reached no clear answer. Nevertheless, it was a welcome break from the paper in front of me.

In the meantime, the cardiganed invigilator went on to write up fifteen-minute increments of time, just like I'd seen on the board. While he did so, Pearls started reading out the exam instructions. You have three hours to complete this exam. You must write three essays. If you require more paper, you must raise your hand. You may begin.

Do it

I opened the exam booklet. Two of the questions for my chosen topics were identical to last years'; I'd written countless essay responses to these questions in the last few weeks. There wasn't a question on my third topic. Suppressing the sickening turn in my stomach, I scoured the questions again. My fourth topic was there, but redesigned in a new question I hadn't come across before. That would be fine. I could do this.

Plan

I circled my three questions. Then I underlined the key words in each one. There. I owned them now. I opened my answer book to the first page and jotted down essay plans for the first two familiar questions, just in case I had a mental block halfway through; after weeks of practice, the plans flowed off my pen like butter off a hot knife. Then I spent a couple of minutes planning out a response to the third, slightly less familiar, question.

I pulled that file of information from my brain, took out the pages, removed a couple, added one or two more and then reordered it to make sense. I had all the information I needed, and I knew exactly where to find it.

Once I had a brief plan for each essay, I put a cross through the page to make sure that my marker couldn't think it was part of my first essay. I checked the clock. Fifteen minutes in. I had a minor panic, then remembered that I'd always spent five minutes planning before each essay in my mock exams at home. This time I'd just done it all at once. No worries.

Write

I started with the least familiar topic. While I had stumbled when reading the question, I flew once I started writing. At the beginning of each paragraph, I looked back to my plan just to make sure that I was on the right track. I'd practised writing so many sentences on this topic that it seemed like nothing at all to reword those sentences to fit this new question. I'd written so many paragraphs over the past few weeks that it felt totally natural to make up a few new ones. I'd used my pen for hours every day, so writing neatly and quickly was second nature.

When I'd finished my conclusion, I took a break. I stretched out my fingers, jiggled my shoulders and had a sip of water. I checked the time. An hour and a quarter in. That meant I had one and three-quarter hours to write my next two essays. Roughly fifty minutes each. I could do this.

I knew my next essay better than the national anthem. My hand ripped back and forth across the paper like a thing possessed. It knew instinctively what to write as it had done so dozens of times before. It did me proud. Then it got cramp.

Overcome the obstacles

I paused mid-paragraph and lay my hand on the table. The fingers were curled up tight like a claw and the palm was quivering; it looked like the sparrow I'd found the day before on the pavement outside our flat, where it had dropped after flying into the lounge window.

Gently, I uncurled the fingers and held them flat against the cool desk. Then I used my good hand to massage the palm. It relaxed. I picked up my pen again and the hand clenched involuntarily. In all the hours I'd spent writing at home, my hand had never done this to me. Now, in the cold light of the exam room, with Pearls squinting down my neck, it was rebelling.

I looked at the clock. I'd spent five minutes dealing with my hand. I tried using my left hand to write. Illegible. There was no other option; if I was going to conquer this exam, I'd have to conquer my right hand. I shook it downwards, three times, as if trying to shake off ants. Pearls squinted harder. With my good hand, I then took the fingers and wrapped them around the pen. I squeezed my fingers on. Whatever happens, I told my hand, you can't let go.

I carried on. My writing wasn't as neat as it had been, and the pain was considerable, but I was able to finish the essay. By my final essay, the cramping had stopped and the hand was left only with a dull ache. I raced through it in thirty minutes, disrupting Pearls three times for extra paper, which she peeled off the pad one sheet at a time slowly enough to make the whole room look up to see where the slow riiiiiip was coming from.

Sit it out

With fifteen minutes to go, I was finished. I read through my work. I edited. I checked to make sure that my name was on everything. Then I sat back to watch everyone else suffering. A girl next to me was staring blankly ahead of her, question booklet unopened. A guy at the end of the row was hyperventilating as he scribbled frantic, oversized words across his page. Another guy down the front was holding his head in his hands. Two-thirds of the class had already left.

Cardigan called out that there were five minutes left. Pearls started staring at her watch. I double-checked my essays. I made sure I'd written my student number down properly. I collected all my sheets together just as Pearl screeched 'TIME!' Pens dropped. People turned to one another, their brows scrunched in pain, their eyes soft with the understanding that they're *just not good at exams.*

Cardigan took my papers and tied them together with a piece of string. I gave him a big smile. 'They don't trust you with a stapler yet, then?'

He scowled and slapped my paper onto the pile in front of him. I laughed. Nothing could bring me down now.

I cycled home in a haze. As soon as I got in the door, I realised how ravenous I was. Three hours of some of the most intense thinking of my life had taken it out of me. I ate three toasties in a row then collapsed on the bed. I woke up four hours later, when Blake got home. He saw me, curled in the foetal position and rushed over.

'Are you okay? How did it go? Was it that awful?'

I unfurled myself like a bird stretching its wings. I smiled.

'Everything went to plan.'

Key exam tips

- Eat a good meal beforehand
- Leave home in plenty of time
- Be on campus half an hour before your exam
- Be outside the exam room ten minutes early (no more, no less)
- Don't drink too much beforehand and always make a toilet stop before going in to the exam room – if you need to go during the exam, one of the examiners will have to escort you out and you'll lose valuable minutes
- Divide your time up by the number of questions you have to answer
- Never forget to answer the question clearly
- Check constantly that you're answering the question
- Use the neatest writing you can
- Always watch the clock
- If you're running out of time, bullet points are better than nothing
- Don't be afraid to ask for extra paper
- Leave every second line blank so that you can add in more information later
- Use arrows and asterisks if you need – your marker will understand the pressure you're under.
- Don't be afraid to ask for water if you run out
- If you get cramp, shake it out and soldier on
- NEVER leave an exam early. Once you've left, there's no going back.

Take a break, then start again

Exams are exhausting. Afterwards, your classmates will probably want to mill about and dissect what they did right and wrong. Hang out with them if you feel like it, but keep exam-talk to a minimum; you did your best and talking about it isn't going to change a thing. Head somewhere you can get something to eat and have a break. If you've got the rest of the day off, spend a couple of hours chilling out. If you've got another exam that day, take half an hour and then get back into it.

Vent to someone who wasn't there. That way you can focus on what you did without them making judgements about it. Be kind to yourself and ask those around you to do the same; you've been through a lot and it's normal to feel spent.

If it's your last exam, go out and celebrate. If you've got more to come, get back to your studies as soon as you can. Your marker is not going to give you extra points for the fact that you had four exams in two days. They are not going to care. It's up to you to make it work, and to excel in all four of them.

If you think you flunked the exam because of something totally unpredicted and out of your control, you should apply for an aegrotat. Accepted scenarios include: a sudden onset of illness, an unexpected event directly before the exam or unacceptable conditions in the exam itself. Get in touch with the head of your department or your lecturer, who'll point you in the right direction.

If you think you flunked the exam because of something within your control, let it go. There's nothing you can do about it. Chances are you didn't do half as badly as you think you did, anyway. My worst exam moment was in a first-year Religious

Studies exam. I reached a question that I had absolutely no idea how to answer so spent half an hour burbling away about something I did know. That one question overshadowed the whole exam and I came out of it convinced that I was going to fail. It turned out that that one question was only worth about 5 per cent and, even then, I'd written enough to get a couple of points. I ended up getting an A for the course.

Get your results

Results night is a psychological phenomenon. Even though I'd have been sure of my success all month, on results day I'd be sure of my failure. I'd spend the afternoon steeling myself for disappointment.

As if sensing this apprehension, uni administration staff always used to release the results at midnight, giving everyone time to get sufficiently hammered and, in doing so, dull their nerves before facing their transcripts. When midnight rolled around and most students found that they hadn't actually failed anything, the alcohol served to intensify their joy. Pre-prepared for a night of celebration or commiseration, most hit the town immediately afterwards.

The results you get on results night (or results day, if that's how your uni works) are your average marks for each course. They are the culmination of all the work you've done during the semester – essays, tests, assignments and, of course, exams – put together and averaged out, depending on the assessment weightings. These are the grades that your future employers will see. They are the symbols of all those late nights of reading, those mad dashes to the essay dropbox, those painful three-hour exams. They are the markers of all you have overcome and all you have achieved.

Step 9
Travel the journey

Your exams are the final requirement of your courses. Once you've got through them all, the first thing you need to do is stop for a moment to celebrate. Take a break. Spend some time with your friends and family and treat yourself to the things you wanted to do when you were stuck inside, sitting your own exams and shutting the world out. After putting all your effort into their lectures, readings, essays and exams, you now own these courses; you've earned the right to keep them forever on your transcript.

Once you've had a moment to celebrate, you need to make a final decision about your next round of courses. As I discovered when I received my first enrolment pack, a BA is not a static 'thing' that you enrol in, chip away at and then complete. It's a changing, personal journey, on which you can only see things with certainty as far as the next lot of courses you've enrolled in. It's a journey on which you can change paths, backtrack and detour, one that you can speed up or slow down according to how tired or energised you feel.

The holidays you get after each exam break are a stopping point for you to look back on the miles you've covered and what you've learnt along the way. Stop and look at how you've changed since the beginning and what you want from the rest of it. Acknowledge how the journey up to this point has shaped you, then start thinking of ways to boost your fitness for the next uphill struggle.

Reassess your courses

If you're part way through the year, you'll probably have enrolled in next semester's courses already. Check to make sure that you're still happy with your selection. If you've changed your mind, give your uni a call or check out their website; most will allow you to submit a request for changes to enrolment online.

If you're at the end of the year, you'll need to choose a whole new set of courses. It's time to go back to your degree sandwich and recraft it in a way that suits what you want *now*. Add some bread by blocking out the first spaces of your timetable with the courses you need to complete your major. Fill in the rest of the gaps with courses that look interesting, useful or easy to you.

Perhaps you've got enough points in another subject to be able to change your major to something different. Perhaps you've decided to go for a double major. Use the skills and experience you've gained so far to reshape your degree how you want.

Change with the times

As you progress through the three levels of a BA, you'll find that you need to enrol in fewer courses at every stopping point. This is because the higher-level your courses are, the more intensive they'll be, so the fewer you'll take at any one time. Where you might have written a 1500-word essay in first year, your second-year lecturers may expect 2500 words and your third-year lecturers 3500. Where you may have been required to reference six articles in your first-year essays, by third year this number may have jumped to ten or twelve.

The primary reason for this is not to make it harder for you. It's to allow you to use the new ways of thinking you've developed along the journey so far to explore concepts more deeply, to engage with theories more intensely, and to incorporate and interact with more viewpoints, possibilities and arguments. The BA structure is designed not to *force* you to think more creatively but to give you the space to do so naturally as you develop your reading, writing and thinking skills.

My first year at uni was the hardest. It was the year I learnt to access and enter the academic world. It was the year I learnt to use the university system to my advantage. It was the year in which I had to address my own fears and insecurities and work out how I was not going to let them get in the way of my success.

After first year, the work got harder but doing it got a lot easier. All the time and effort I'd invested into getting good habits, overcoming my fears and training my brain started to pay off. Although each subsequent year posed a new set of challenges and a new system of rules and norms to be learnt and practised, the fundamental culture of the place remained the same.

The habits and strategies I developed in first year set me up for the rest of my degree. With these as my foundation, the other changes happened naturally. For example, I used the same essay-crafting process right through uni, but each year my writing naturally became more fluid and my insights more perceptive. I used the same exam study strategy, but each year I found that I was able to write clearer and more developed answers. I kept up my good reading habits but naturally started reading more widely and more adventurously with each year.

While you'll naturally develop as a scholar, make sure that this is happening at the expected speed. Read the assessment criteria carefully at each level and take note of how you're expected to perform differently as you go. Keep in close contact with your lecturers about how your writing is progressing. If you feel at any stage as if you're out of your depth, GET HELP. Support services aren't just for first years.

Check your workload as you go

Learning is a process, not an event – something that happens in its own time rather than when you want it to. The average BA takes three years to complete – this represents the amount of time it takes for most students to progress through the three levels of learning a BA offers, understanding the key ideas and developing their own responses as they do so. While the whole BA is a process of learning, so too is each course within it; most lecturers spend the whole length of the course getting you to a point at which you're ready to move on to the next learning challenge.

While three years is the recommended timeframe for a BA, it's not a compulsory one. Most universities offer the possibility of studying for your BA part time, and therefore taking a bit longer to complete it – this can be a useful option if you're working or have kids and can't fit a full-time schedule of lectures into your day. Likewise, it's possible to complete your degree in under three years – mine was all over in two.

Consider summer study

Much can be achieved during the long three months of summer. Many use this time to relax, take up hobbies or develop their social lives. Others use it to earn money to help them pay back their student loans. I used it to cut down the amount I needed to pay back. By using the summer months to get a couple more courses under my belt, I knocked months off my degree. I'd do a bit more working and a bit more relaxing than usual, but study remained my main occupation.

Summer school was the best time of my uni life. For a start, it's warm so finding the motivation to get out of bed and cycle across town is a lot easier. Secondly, it's quiet, so finding parking places, books in the library or time to speak with a lecturer are more straightforward. Thirdly, there's a higher proportion of ambitious and engaged students, making class discussion more interesting and providing more opportunities to make good friends. Fourthly, the range of courses is more limited but often more quirky, pushing you in to interesting courses you might not have usually considered. Fifthly – and most importantly – because courses are only five or ten weeks long, they are more intensive; this means that you can only take one at a time, allowing you to get fully immersed in its content rather than having to share your attention between three or four courses at one time.

So, while uni management will be quick to warn you about the heavy workload, my experience was that summer school courses were far easier to manage than regular courses. Bear in mind, though, that some universities have already begun to scale back their summer school options, the rationale being that three months is not enough time for complex concepts to be fully grasped and explored. (That cutting summer courses also significantly cuts costs is less freely disclosed.)

Whatever the reason, these cuts mean that if you're interested in summer school you'd be unwise to factor it in to your planning at the beginning of the year; keep your eyes open at the end of the year for any summer school opportunities and, if there are some that interest you, reconsider your plan then.

Work at your own speed

Perhaps my workload was more taxing than other students' but it was all I had ever known of university. With nine hours of study a day and two or three weeks of holiday per year, my job as a student was comparable to the paid jobs I'd had in the past. There was nothing unusual to me about setting my alarm at 7.30 a.m. to be ready to start my study at 8, or in calling home to say I'd be late because I'd been held up working on an assignment. Having experienced the pressures of full-time work meant that I quickly adapted to my new full-time, all-year role as a student.

I don't recommend that you shorten your degree. The three years have been specified for good reason and, what's more, it's simply not possible at many universities to increase your workload above the recommended level. I was only allowed to do it because by the start of my second year I was getting consistently good marks. Plus, with four summer school courses factored into my degree, I only needed one course over the standard workload to complete my degree in the second year.

In any case, the workload of my first year at university was totally normal. This was the most challenging year and I simply couldn't have taken on any more work and still improved as much as I did. Stick with the recommended number of courses in your first year then evaluate at the end of the year according to how well you've coped with the pressures, how you'd like the remainder of your time at uni to look and what the summer school options are like.

Step 10
Use it

Although there will be times when it doesn't feel like it, there is an end to your BA. Sometime after you've read a small library's worth of literature, mastered too many essays to count and conquered more exams than you'd care to think about, you will achieve the number of points required to get a BA. You will sit your final exam and walk back across uni for the last time as an undergraduate. You will glance back at the now familiar buildings and hardly believe that you could have got so lost in them during your early days as a first-year student.

Although your study may be over, the journey of your BA is not. Remember your initial reason for getting this degree? The journey of your BA goes on for as long as you are fulfilling that reason. When you see your BA in this way – as a lifelong journey – it puts the huge investment you've made in getting it into perspective.

Fulfilling the dreams you had for your BA at the beginning is going to take time. Just like learning, the fulfillment of your reason to get a BA is going to be a process rather than an event. Encourage it along but don't force it; there's no need to rush into things. You've been meeting deadlines for three years now. It's time to slow down for a while.

Enjoy it

Celebrate. Get your friends and family to join you. Tell them how hard you've worked for your BA. Show them how proud you are to have made it. Go to every ceremony, party or ball designed to honour your achievement.

My graduation in December was one of the proudest moments of my life. Blake and I spent the morning racing around Christchurch, taking photos of me in my regalia at every scenic point we came to. Me under a tree. Me next to our Cambridge Terrace flat. Me using my robe as a cape. We went to university and I paced the halls and rooms in my big robe and silly hat, feeling like a million dollars. I dropped in on my lecturers and got photos with them, too.

My epiphany came at the top of the library staircase, as I was waiting for Blake to take the next photo. From my vantage point I could see at least five floors of books. In between the shelves were students hunched over laptops. I could see librarians scuttling about between the artifacts. I could see people rifling through the archives. I could see the regal University of Canterbury flag hanging off the banister. I was a graduate of this place. I'd done it.

Even though I was only one of hundreds getting my degree that day, the crowd cheered just for me as I came out onto the stage. I shook the Archbishop's hand and took my degree then turned to face the crowd. I paused for just long enough to throw a smile towards Dad, Granddad and Blake, who were watching from the wings. As I walked down the steps, I could see Dr Matheson at the end of the aisle. He held up both thumbs and grinned.

Take a break

Don't rush into anything. Chill out for a second. Take some time out to recover. Do something different for a few weeks. You've been in the same routine for a number of years now and it's going to take your brain a while to adjust.

Right after my degree, I went to Tonga. I stayed in a flat right on the beach with no access to shops, bars or restaurants. I lay on the beach and read trashy novels with no literary merit. I didn't think about anything at all beyond my next meal. It was perfect.

Canvas your options

You've basically got five. The first is to do nothing. The second is to get a temporary job, something to keep you going until you work out what you want to do. The third is to get the kind of job that will put you on track towards the career you want. The fourth is to enrol in further study. The fifth is to travel.

The only question you need to ask yourself is 'How can I *best* use what I've learnt during my BA *now*?' Only you can decide this one.

After meeting the requirements of my degree, my first course of action was getting out of uni and into a temporary job. By the end of my degree, the constant pressure of essay after essay after exam was starting to wear me down. I couldn't wait to leave the place. I left in November 2008 swearing never to set foot in a university again.

My scholarship offers came in the mail shortly afterwards: a UC Senior Scholarship, awarded on merit by the University of Canterbury academic board; and a John Connal Scholarship, awarded for Excellence in English. I wrote a thank you reply to each, in which I politely declined the free postgrad study. Nothing could distract me from my overwhelming need to *use* the skills I'd developed during my degree in the *real world*. While my BA had taught me a lot about the way the world worked, it had taught me far more about the way *I* worked, and all I wanted was to use this knowledge to experience the world.

Studying, though, from what I can tell, is like childbirth. Straight after giving birth, most women vow never to put themselves through such an ordeal again. A year or two down the track, once the pain of the moment has faded, most go back and do it again. It's called the survival instinct and I believe that education is as instinctual as reproduction. Those of us who make it to uni are drawn there because we know it is key to our development. We want to honour the advances of our parents by bettering them and we want to mould ourselves into role models for our children to aspire beyond.

After a couple of months of working in 'the real world', I was missing university. My second course of action was to go back. In January, the Mass Communication department contacted me to ask if I'd like to return as a tutor. I accepted and returned to uni in February 2009. For me, there was no better first way to use my degree than to help others with theirs. Although I didn't realise it at the time, it was a key stage in my journey to becoming a teacher.

In June 2009, I used my BA to travel. My experience of the world post-BA was totally different from my pre-grad OE. Where pre-grad I'd seen beautiful landmarks and met wonderful people, as a graduate I saw stories and debates, stereotypes and contradictions. Where before I'd asked 'When?' and 'Where?', now I was asking 'Why?' and 'How?'. Every town posed a new challenge to my intellect, every government a new chance to question my morals and values, every person a story by which to make better sense of my own. I must have been infuriating to travel with.

Cambodia showed me that I wanted to use my BA to teach. Four weeks into the country, Blake and I took a trip on a lawnmower-motor-propelled barge across Tonle Sap, the largest freshwater lake in Southeast Asia. After a couple of hours of chugging through villages with houses on stilts, pig pens and gardens, our driver dropped us off at a jetty so that we could stretch our legs and check out a nearby temple. We were met by a young monk of about fifteen, who introduced himself as the spiritual leader and teacher of the region; his side job as an impromptu tour guide had left him with fairly good English that, like most Cambodians, he was keen to practise with us.

As we wandered down the pathway leading up to the temple, about a dozen children came running out from the foliage and began waving so hard I feared that their tiny wrists would snap. Our guide smiled and said something in Khmer to them. He turned to me.

'I am teacher to many.'

I gave one little girl a wave back. 'How many do you teach?'

'Everyone in village – maybe sixty, maybe seventy.'

'How old are they?'

He thought for a while then, failing to find the words, demonstrated by holding his outstretched palm about two feet from the ground, and then lifting it up beyond his head.

'So what do you teach them?'

'I teach them the stories of the Buddha. I teach them about the lake. I teach them some English. Many children want to go university.'

'So why are you the only teacher?'

He laughed. 'I only one who know English! I only one who can read books! Everyone want to learn, but no one practise. Cambodia once have many educated people but Khmer Rouge . . .' – searching for the word, he extended a finger and drew it sharply across his throat. 'Now everyone wants education, but no one can teach it. I learn off the foreigner, and I teach to the children.'

I understood. The driver hadn't brought us here to see the temple. He'd brought us here to teach the monk, who'd been charged with the impossible task of educating the village without having had an education himself. Without access to books, TV or the internet, the monk had started using foreigners as his education. The education that I'd been flaunting like the latest rucksack (every traveller should have one) was to the locals a chance for freedom, an opportunity to defy a horrendous past, a symbol of hope and possibility.

The monk showed us around the temple and then took us to a riverside hut.

He handed us each a can of soft drink. 'I show you my temple. I give you drink. I don't ask for money. I ask that you sit here for some time and answer some of my question.'

We sat with him for at least an hour as he withdrew sample after sample of writing for us to read and comment on. He peered over our shoulders as we read, pointing his long fingernail towards areas of concern. 'This right?', 'This part?', 'How to say this?'

He was still asking questions as our rickety barge shunted away from the riverbank. We yelled back answers until it became too hard to hear. As we backed away, children began to emerge from the nearby foliage to join him at the water's edge. By the time we turned around the first bend in the river, there must have been twenty or thirty of them there, waving hard enough to shake their hands right off their arms.

By the time I got back to New Zealand in June 2010, I had enrolled in the University of Canterbury's teacher training programme. I knew what I wanted to do. I had found the sort of job I'd wanted but not been qualified enough to apply for before I'd enrolled at uni.

Keep in touch

As much as you may want to break away from uni, it pays to keep some ties. Your carefully forged relationships with your lecturers don't end when you get your degree. In fact, once you become a certified academic, they may even become more rewarding: you are part of the academic world now and your lecturers, though still guides, are closer to peers than they ever were when you were an undergrad.

Lecturers are great people to know. Not only are they smart, interesting people who are always up for a debate, they're also influential. People with letters after their names make great referees, but you can't expect them to want to support you unless you put some effort in yourself. Flick your lecturers an email from time to time. Pop in to their office and say hello if you're passing by campus. They'll be thrilled to see you.

Remember your debts

Oh yeah. That loan you took out at the beginning of your degree? You've got to start paying it back now.

Never forget your achievement

You've reached the end of the pool. Here, have a towel. Sit with me on this bench and take a moment to look back on the incredible feat you've just achieved. Watch the trembling newbies at the top of the diving board. Remember when that was you? Watch the swimmers struggling to catch their breath at the half-way mark. Remember how that felt? Watch as some put their wet hands on the edges of the pool, ready to haul themselves out, unable to continue. Remember when you considered doing the same?

Wave to the few people scattered around the sidelines who are applauding you. Your supporters have been great. Acknowledge what they've said to inspire you, what they've done to make your life easier, what they've thought about you to give you confidence in yourself.

Remember, though, that in the most breathless, painful moments, you were on your own. You may have been encouraged by others, but what propelled you forward was your own determination to achieve your goal. Your degree is the product of this determination. It represents the fact that you know what you want, and you are prepared to do what it takes to get it. It is a marker of your commitment, energy and ambition.

This is why a BA is such an asset in the twenty-first century. It signifies what you've learnt but, more importantly, it signifies why you've learnt it; it shows the world that you are someone who loves to learn. Your transcript is evidence not just of what you know but also of your ability to question what you know, to argue for and against it, to view it from multiple perspectives, to accept that it is all relative.

Your BA is more than a qualification. It is a marker of your identity. Add it to your CV, hang it on your wall, put its letters after your name as a symbol of who you are.

Acknowledgements

Thanks to the people who've seen this project through from the beginning: Blake Dawson, for supporting me as a nerdy student and first-time author; Donald Matheson, for showing me why and how to get this published; and Philip Armstrong, for being enthusiastic from the outset.

Thanks to Maggie Jury, Ian Jury, Graham Jury and Dennis Jury for taking education seriously; Julia Dawson, for providing a roof and a laptop when I needed them; Steve Langley, for supporting my writing since high school; Tina Mackie, for listening since the first draft; and the boys of Rongotai College for keeping me grounded about what students need.

Thanks to the University of Canterbury for introducing me to the BA: all my lecturers who had souls, my tutors, my classmates who excelled and struggled, and the students on whom I trialled my first ideas.

Finally, a massive thanks to the team at Auckland University Press for publishing my first book in such a supportive, positive way: Sam Elworthy, for being excited about it from the start; Anna Hodge, for reading and re-reading, commenting and re-commenting; Ginny Sullivan for copy editing; Katrina Duncan for designing; and Christine O'Brien for marketing.

The quotations on pages 60, 61 and 64 by Eoin Devereux from *Understanding the Media* (2nd edition, 2007) and the text on pages 37–38 by Boaventura de Sousa Santos from 'Globalizations' (*Theory, Culture and Society*, vol. 23, no. 2–3, May 2006) are reproduced by permission of Sage Publications. Quotations on pages 59 and 60 by D. K. Thussu from *International Communication: Continuity and Change* (2nd edition, 2006) © Bloomsbury Academic. The line by Ronald Bettig and Jeanne Hall from 'All the News that Fits: The News and Advertising Industries' (*Big Media, Big Money*, 2003) cited on pages 116, 118 and 119 is used with the permission of Rowman & Littlefield Publishers.

The COMS102 essay question is reproduced with the permission of Jim Tully, Head of the School of Social and Political Sciences, University of Canterbury; and the SOCI111 essay questions by permission of Michael Grimshaw, Acting Programme Coordinator, Sociology, University of Canterbury. The quotation by Joe Bennett is used by permission. Philip Armstrong, Blake Dawson, Maggie Jury, Donald Matheson, Ryan Wood and Youthline have all given permission for their appearances here and for the retelling of their stories. All writing reflects the opinions of the author and not the opinions of the University of Canterbury, Rongotai College, Youthline, or any other organisation or person mentioned in this book.

Quick look-up

BLAKE DAWSON

Rebecca Jury graduated with a BA in English and Mass Communication from the University of Canterbury in 2008 with an excellent grade average. Since completing her degree she has worked as a university tutor, a youth counsellor and, most recently, a high school teacher. *BA: An Insider's Guide* is her first book. A blog to accompany the book can be found at www.aninsidersguide.com.

Rebecca came up with the idea of a study guide in the final year of her BA, when she saw that many of her peers were still developing skills to cope with the demands of tertiary study. She produced a small study skills leaflet for distribution among friends and fellow students, which became this guide.

Alongside writing, Rebecca enjoys cooking, travelling and trying to keep old cars on the road.